# ABOUT THE BOOK

This book is about living and working in a mobile army surgical hospital (MASH) in South Vietnam. It talks about the hospital itself, the setting, how we lived, how we coped with less-than-good circumstances, the type of patients we received, the equipment we worked with, and the emotional highs and lows that were part of every day. The stories are true. Some of the dates and numbers of things may be off a little; that was a long time ago. Names have not been used to protect the wonderful, dedicated people with whom I worked and lived.

# 2D Surgical Hospital

# 2D Surgical Hospital

An Khe to Chu Lai South Vietnam

Lorna Griess

Rev. date: 11/17/2017

**To order additional copies of this book, contact:**
Xlibris
1-888-795-4274
www.Xlibris.com
Orders@Xlibris.com
742513

# CONTENTS

# FOREWORD

This book is about my experience living and working in a war zone -South Vietnam. I have written this book because the question I get most often, in a very hesitant voice, is "What is it like, you know, being in a war?" "Is it scary?" There is no short answer for that question. I usually answer with something that agrees with what they just said. "Yes, it was pretty scary sometimes."

When I think about it, there is no way to explain it to someone who has not been there. People watch war movies and think they understand, but, they don't. Think about all the normal things you do every day, routinely. You shower, blow-dry your hair, eat breakfast, and choose an outfit to wear for whatever you are going to do. You go out in your car, have a burger at Wendy's for lunch, drive home, eat dinner and watch your favorite TV show, and then go to bed at your usual time.

In a war zone, all that normalcy, plus the security of knowing you can sleep safely and comfortably all night, is gone. Sometimes you get so tired that sleep overwhelms you until you are called to work again. You are camping out with a group of people you barely know, in a strange land, and being asked to use your skills in unusual and sometimes crisis situations. Over time, you seek a new normal out of the chaos, and the old normal fades. The comfort, security, and friends are gone. You create a new world with friends who share the experience. Often, you can run the entire range of emotions in a short period of time. It feels like an emotional roller coaster. You grow and change. You quickly find out who you are and what you can handle. Most of the time you are pleased; sometimes it is not pretty. You learn quickly and hope you are enough for what you are called to do.

Yes, living and working in a war zone is scary. It is also heartwarming, fun, educational, sad, heartbreaking, fatiguing, and energizing. It is something you will remember all of your life.

Coming home was the hard part.

# ACKNOWLEDGMENTS

Many have contributed ideas, editing, and encouragement to this manuscript. I would especially like to thank members of my writers club, Mary Weins, Cynthia Martin, Maureen Caputo, Lita Lappin, and Michele Shimek, for their suggestions and support during the planning and initial outline of the book. I would also like to thank Vernon Renwanz for the time he spent editing and Sandra Hanes for the time she spent listening and helping me sort pictures. It is a special challenge to write a book about a combat hospital for a civilian audience. Last but not least, I would like to thank Joseph C. Caputo II for the hours he spent converting my forty-year-old slides to digital prints.

# CHAPTER 1

## Travis Air Force Base, California

My heart pounded wildly as I got out of the car at the Travis air terminal. I tried very hard to give the impression that this was just another day in the life of an Army nurse. That was useless. I was plain scared. I was leaving behind everything I knew and going to war in Vietnam. This was not a practice exercise, this was real. I got my duffel bag and makeup case out of the trunk, said goodbye to my family, and turned toward the terminal. During the short walk, I was able to regain my confidence and stride through the door looking and feeling like a nurse on a mission. I was a First Lieutenant looking sharp in my green uniform with skirt, nylons, polished black pumps, black regulation handbag with shoulder strap and flat garrison hat. This was 1966, and women's uniforms, except for utility uniforms, did not include pantsuits. Fatigues would have been much more comfortable.

During the walk, I reflected on how I got here. I was twenty-eight years old, six years out of nursing school. I had served two years in the Navy at Newport Rhode Island Naval Hospital, during the Cuban Missile Crisis and decided I did not like Navy life because, at the time, women were not allowed on ships and there were very few places to go in the world. I got off of active duty into the inactive reserves. Instead of going home to California, I moved to New York City. The World's Fair was going to open soon, and I wanted to see it.

New York City was fun. I worked on the seventeenth floor of Cornell Medical Center and learned a lot. But I was getting restless. After a year of enjoying New York, I went home to Sacramento, California. I worked at a local hospital for a while, still restless. I missed the camaraderie and excitement of military life. The news was carrying a lot about the war in Vietnam and how it was escalating. I went to see the Army recruiter, he sent me to see the nurse recruiter in San

Francisco, and she completed the paperwork to change my status from Navy Reserve to Army Reserve. In a short time, I was off to San Antonio, Texas, for basic officer training specific for nurses, doctors and other medical personnel, for six weeks, then on to Fitzsimons Army Medical Center in Denver to await orders for Vietnam. They arrived in three short months.

In addition to the orders, I had to make out my will and sign a letter acknowledging that if our unit were to be captured by the enemy, I would be left to care for the injured men, and I would be rescued with the men. There would be no special attempt to rescue me first because I am female.

When the door at the terminal closed behind me with a whoosh, I snapped back to reality, and fear became energy. Inside, the room was filled with men also in green uniforms. They were standing, sitting, or lying on duffel bags waiting for flights to somewhere. Most were on my flight. I pulled out my orders which served as Army travel documents and lugged my heavy duffel bag and carry-on makeup case to the long line at the check-in window. I was excited to see Ellie and Betty, two nurses from my basic class, already in line. They had orders to the same place. We were going to Second Surgical Hospital, designated as 2d SURG, a MASH (Mobile Army Surgical Hospital) Unit in An Khe, located in the central highlands of South Vietnam. The line progressed slowly as we chatted. We checked in finally. Our duffel bags were taken and tagged and put in a pile with the others. All were the same size, shape, and color. Miraculously, none were lost.

The three of us found a place to lean in the crowded room while we waited for our flight. A plane arrived and discharged passengers into the terminal. Every one of them wore disheveled fatigues, looked battle-worn, and smelled like a mixture of mildew and something unidentifiable. I had a bad feeling that I knew where their flight originated and that I would be able to identify that smell soon. That plane left, and before long a shiny Continental jet pulled up to the gate with the usual hiss of engines and brakes. My heart leapt a little. Our flight was called, and we boarded. This was a chartered jet configured for troop movements, which only meant that they found a way to add more seats. We wedged ourselves in with our knees touching the seats ahead and got ready for what was going to be a long flight. The three of us were the only women on board. I quietly said goodbye to California with a mixture of excitement, sadness, and terror.

The first stop was Honolulu, My first trip to Hawaii. The view was great - from the airplane. We could get up and stretch, but we could not leave the aircraft. As we got seated again, the plane taxied to the runway and we said goodbye to Honolulu. Next stop was Manila, the Philippines. This was getting exciting. I was now flying into mysterious places I had only heard or read about. My uncle had been a Navy baker on a ship during WWII. He would tell my sister and me stories about the far-away places he had been, and he sent us gifts. I remember hula skirts from Hawaii and brightly colored. silk kimonos from Japan.

Hours later, the flight was getting long, the space tight, the uniform - smaller and uncomfortable, the shoes dropped to the floor, as feet swelled, and sleep was off and on, with plenty of head bobs. The stewards and stewardesses worked quietly to serve enough food and drinks to keep us alive and hydrated. When we crossed the international dateline, the pilot made an announcement and there was a brief murmur of voices. The plane was too full for any grand celebration, but I noted another first in my life.

The pilot announced our arrival at Clark AFB in the Philippines. We had to circle the airport for about thirty minutes because a Filipino fighter jet had crashed and the runway needed to be cleared. We landed just to refuel for the final leg of the trip into Saigon. Again, we were allowed to stand up and move around in the narrow, crowded aisle, but we could not leave the aircraft. Altogether, we spent at least twenty-four hours on this airplane and ended up with wrinkled clothes, swollen feet, mossy teeth and airplane seat hair. Everyone was the same mess. In retrospect, I will never know why we were sent to war wearing office attire. Fatigues would have been a blessing. It could have been because Saigon was swarming with VIPs, and the troops in Saigon wore Class A uniforms (green suits). The nurses in the Field Hospital in Saigon wore white uniforms, so we had to show up looking nice. If you can call a rumpled mess "looking nice."

The plane finally lifted off the tarmac at Clark AFB, and we were on our final leg into Saigon. I was alert now and staring out the window because there was something to see - islands. The flight was fairly short, so before long the pilot announced our arrival at Ton Son Nut, but we would have to circle the airport for a while because a Vietnamese fighter had crashed and the runway needed to be cleared. Two in a row left me feeling a little uneasy.

Our landing was uneventful. The plane emptied its passengers into the terminal in a great mob and left. There were signs directing this huge mass of people into orderly lines for bag pickup and destinations. When we got off of the air-conditioned plane, we entered a steam bath of heat and humidity.

The terminal was no better. It had a rattling air conditioner and ceiling fans that could not handle the humidity or the heat. The constantly open doors did not help. The uniform that was merely uncomfortable was now deadly. My feet just barely fit back into the shoes I had kicked off hours ago. Our flight upcountry was scheduled for the next morning, so we boarded a bus for the BOQs (Bachelor Officers Quarters), to stay the night. Our bags, by some miracle, were aboard the bus. We had arrived safely.

The bus, well, van, had a very cheerful young driver who kept up a running dialog about the area as he drove. We left the airport and bumped and merged into tiny, cobblestoned streets along with an eclectic collection of small cars, pedicabs, bicycles, scooters, and trucks - all of whom were honking horns for right of way. I was way too tired to be scared as we wound our way through neighborhoods of white stucco homes with eye-level stucco walls surrounding them and trees poking up behind them. We passed busy outdoor markets with strange hanging items of food and flies buzzing all over. We entered a gate and pulled up in front of a nice-looking hotel with a porch, flower pots, and chairs outside. I don't remember very much of my stay in Saigon because it was short and I was tired, and a little numb from the trip. We checked in and were directed toward our rooms, but instructed not to drink the water coming out of the faucets. My room was small and hot, with a ceiling fan that limped along at a slow speed. It also had an assortment of large, ugly insects that were, as I would soon learn, endemic and ever-present in Vietnam. I hated bugs! I was more afraid of them than the enemy. That changed as the year progressed.

I was starting to get an idea of what "leaving behind everything I knew" meant. I was still okay with that, but I had a lot to learn. I had to learn to live and thrive with a "new normal". For starters, gone was running potable water in the house, air conditioning, television, fast food, my own car for transportation (which meant independence), and family and friends available by telephone (mass market cell phones did not exist). This list would grow as time passed.

Later, Ellie, Betty, and I met for dinner at the cafeteria in the hotel/BOQ. I don't remember what dinner was, but afterward we joined a group of men in the lounge who were also in transit and talked and sang folk songs for a couple of hours. That seems a little strange now because the songs were almost all anti-war. That was October 1966, and that's what was popular. Emotion was running high. I did not really have an identifiable emotion; it was more of a roller coaster. I was glad to be finished with the long trip, homesick, excited to be there, and scared all at the same time. We all had flights out the next morning, so we went our separate ways, to very hot rooms and went to bed. I was tired enough that the bugs did not bother me. I woke up early, cleaned up, put the uniform back on, gathered my belongings, and met the others for breakfast, then waited for transportation back to the airport.

The same van that picked us up the previous day was back with the same driver to take us back to Ton Son Nut. He was as cheerful as he was the day before, and we got the same scenic tour down cobblestone streets mixing with anything with wheels and a horn.

Ton Son Nut was a major embarking place for incoming personnel and VIPs who came and went. We showed our orders, surrendered our duffel bags, and were directed to a gate down a corridor. This was a major airport, but it had no ramps for passengers. You walked out to the airplane and up the stairs. Our transportation was an Army workhorse called a C-130. It was propeller-driven, wide and clumsy-looking, but it could land on a very short metal runway called PSP (pierced Steel Plank), which was most of the runways upcountry. From the sky, the runways looked like Band-Aids. They were portable, metal and full of holes, but they stood up through rain and mud, enemy attacks, and heavy aircraft take-offs and landings. If damaged, they were easy to repair.

Wheels up again, we headed north to An Khe and our final destination in the central highlands. The plane was not full, so we had a chance to relax and look around. I looked out the window to see a beautiful landscape of farms, lush green countryside, and small villages. After an hour or so, the pilot came on and announced the "fasten seat belts" routine, not that they were ever unfastened, and thatwe were about to land (C-130s do not have flight attendants). I looked down at the Band-Aid on the ground and shut my eyes, hoping the pilot could at least hit it with some degree of accuracy. He did, effortlessly, and we were on the ground.

# CHAPTER 2

## Welcome to Second Surg.

The portable stairway was pushed up to the side of the C-130. As the doors were manually opened, we all got up to gather our belongings. I stepped out onto the top of the stairs and immediately felt the fresh coolness that comes from rain. It had just rained a lot. Puddles were everywhere. I looked around beyond the runway and saw an assortment of Army green tents, Quonset huts, dirt roads, and wire fences. There was a large mountain with communication gear on top straight ahead. The place looked pretty bleak but blended into the landscape. I walked down the stairs and headed for the Quonset hut that was the "terminal." The bags were unloaded and met us at the terminal. We checked in and did not have long to wait before a vehicle marked "2d Surg" pulled up outside to pick us up. We piled in, bags were tossed into the back, and off we went. I looked at the bareness of my new home and had no opinion, the situation was too new. The vehicle passed a sign that said "2d Surg" and pulled up beside a large tent, that turned out to be headquarters. A very cheerful man in fatigues came running out to meet us, introduced himself as the company clerk, and said "Welcome to Second Surg."

We got out, I am sure, looking very new because the clerk started talking non-stop, as we walked toward headquarters. He talked about the hospital, how great it was, and what we had to do. To this day I do not remember what he said. What I do remember is that a plane, he said an Army Caribou, had crashed against Hong Kong Mountain (the mountain behind the hospital) the afternoon before, and there were still casualties in the hospital. It had been landing and missed the runway, so it had been going slowly. No one was killed. One man had been positioned so that on impact an M-16 had been pushed through his abdomen and out the back, making a hole in his pelvic bone. He was doing well now. The clerk also said that we controlled the top of the mountain - it was a communication station - and we controlled the bottom, but the Viet Cong controlled the middle. I did not need to hear this. During this time, the vehicle driver was unloading our duffel bags. The bags were dropped on the ground, end down, right into a mud puddle. Deep puddles were everywhere, so they were hard to miss. The bottom of the bag did not thoroughly dry the whole year I was there. This was my birthday - October 5, 1966.

We entered the dimly lit tent and gave the clerk our set of orders assigning us to Second Surgical Hospital. He continued his spiel as he gave us predetermined places to live - an empty Quonset hut in the hospital area. The rest of the nurses lived in a tent across the dirt utility road, but the tent did not have room for three people at the moment so we had temporary quarters, that turned into long-term. At first I was disappointed. Then I realized that we were actually lucky. The Quonset hut had a floor, was more weatherproof, and controlled the bugs somewhat.

We were shown to our quarters to settle in and given a brief orientation about where the important things were - the latrine, an outhouse with a sign saying "women," the mess hall, and what dinner hours were. A tour would be scheduled for the next day. I looked around the good-sized Quonset hut and chose a bed. Each of us had a hospital-type bed, a locker with a few hangers, and a bedside stand with a drawer and a lower compartment. With a huge sigh of relief, I took off my green uniform with skirt, nylons, polished black pumps, flat garrison hat, and stylish black handbag with shoulder strap and put on something more comfortable. I did bring some civilian clothing. I later found out that what we thought were crude living accommodations, the men thought were great. They were very proud of what they put together for the new female nurses. It is only a matter of perspective. Mine changed radically as time moved on.

Privacy was a luxury. None of the doors had locks. There was no running water anywhere unless it was a jerry-rigged set-up in the operating room and/or mess hall. I was still excited to be here and unpacked my soggy duffel bag into the furniture I had available.

The next morning we would meet the Chief Nurse and get the tour and our assignments. Such as it was, I was home.

Hong Kong Mountain

# CHAPTER 3

## Second Surgical Hospital

With the new day came a freshness of attitude, excitement, and comfortable clothes. I put on clean but mildly creased fatigues with sewed-on, subdued or blackened insignia. The hospital area was a no-hat, no-salute zone. Enemy snipers looked for bright officer brass or for who was being saluted and had fun picking them off. I shook off that thought and joined Ellie and Betty for the walk to breakfast.

Breakfast was a treat. The aroma of frying sausages filled the air. As we entered the "mess hall," we created quite a stir. Heads turned, voices quieted, feet shifted. Everyone looked at the new nurses but tried not to stare. Many of them eventually approached our table and said hello. The food was buffet style, you get in line and pick up a metal tray. I had sausages, scrambled eggs, toast, and coffee. In the fresh air it was delicious. The food was called "B rations." The food was freeze dried, packaged and reconstituted for cooking. The canned "C rations" were used in the field. The hospital only used "C rations" when something in the kitchen was broken. It was said that hospitals needed better food because patients were healing. I did not argue.

Breakfast over, the three of us headed for headquarters and our meeting with the Chief Nurse. She was a slim, blonde major with her long hair in a bun. She welcomed us cheerfully but looked very tired. She was due to go home in less than three months. We got a briefing on what the hospital did, the types of patients we would see, and general comments about expectations. Shifts for work were twelve hours long, six days a week. We learned that since Vietnam was a malaria zone, we would be taking CP pills (Chloroquin-Primaquin) pills once a week for malaria prevention. Laundry of fatigues would be done by a Vietnamese contractor off-post for a nominal cost. Telephones were almost nonexistent except in headquarters. We had the old crank-type field phone that only an expert could use. The last item was Script. We did not use the US dollar for purchases; we traded it for script, or "funny money." With questions, the briefing lasted over an hour. Afterward, we got our assignments. I was assigned to the recovery room/intensive care unit (RR/ICU). She turned us over to the senior NCO (sergeant), and we started off on the tour of our new home.

During the tour we got a lot of friendly kidding because we looked new and brought a touch of home. Anyone we met with less than three months to go in country were short-timers. Some of them would create a calendar by making a walking stick and cutting an inch off every day, until it was too short to use. Others had a wall calendar and would X off the days as they passed. The favorite saying was: "You are so new that by the time you go home, a bridge will be built to San Francisco." During the last couple of months in country, some people became very careful. Many people lost their lives by being careless for a second. There is no "do over" in a war zone.

The tour took us to meet all the key people and see all the key places. The hospital sat on the base camp of the First Air Cavalry Division. It was at the base of Hong Kong Mountain, the mountain I saw when I got off of the C - 130. Because the hospital was near the base of the mountain, the ground it sat on sloped gently down-hill. The ground was rocky, with a lot of loose dirt. The hospital had most of the things a hospital at home would have, only smaller and mobile. It had about one hundred beds, an emergency or triage area, an operating room with six operating areas, a recovery room/ICU, a central material section (CMS) where all the equipment was cleaned and sterilized, and three wards for recovering patients. It had a lab that did some basic blood work, nothing major, an x-ray department with portable machines, and an area to develop the film. This was a small town. It also had a post office, a mess hall or dining facility, dental clinic, chapel, small PX (post exchange), laundry facilities, and motor pool. There was no running water anywhere, but water buffalos (white barrels sitting on legs with a faucet on one end) were sitting all around the compound for people to draw water when needed. The hospital also had electricity, generated from somewhere on the compound.

A dirt road curved around the hospital area for utility vehicles. This was a constant source of dust or mud. The road was in sort of a horseshoe shape with the curve up hill. The hospital wards were in Quonset huts with air conditioning in the OR and RR/ICU only. There were covered walkways between the buildings. The personnel lived in tents across the dirt road from the hospital. Four people had small tents by themselves. The Hospital Commander, the XO

(Executive Officer), the Chief Nurse and the Command Sargent Major. The rest of the staff lived in large tents sectioned off into personal areas. Doctors had a tent as did nurses. When I was there, all doctors were men and all nurses were women. Officer country was on the left side of the hospital and Enlisted on the right. Each had its own shower facility and recreational facility. Ours was called the 19$^{th}$ hole. Great place for spending off duty hours.

Our small PX had a lot of items like a small store. Most were for men. The Chief Nurse finally explained to the very embarrassed store clerk about the things women needed -like sanitary napkins and he managed to stock some of those for emergencies, but I don't think he ever really understood the concept. For the most part, all the things that I needed, laundry soap, sanitary supplies, shampoo, light bulbs, etc. were sent from home. My mother got very good at packing so the items would go through the Army mail service (I called the APO blender) without breaking. The PX did get a few items like cameras and film, stereo equipment, binoculars and uniform replacement items. It also sold regulation "jungle boots." We arrived with all leather black boots that tend to get hot in the summer. The jungle boots were canvas and leather.

By definition, a MASH unit is designed to be small, mobile, and positioned near the FEBA (forward edge of the battle area). Vietnam did not have a FEBA, the war was everywhere. The hospital was designed and equipped to take life and limb saving surgery patients only. The theory being, the sooner a soldier got to a medical treatment facility, the better his chances of survival. The theory is absolutely true even today. The problem occurs when a helicopter pilot goes into the battle areas he is usually under fire. He does not triage the patients, nor should he, he picks up everybody on the ground needing help and leaves quickly. We got all kinds of patients: surgical, Vietnamese civilians including children, medical, psychiatric and so forth. We had to be ready for whatever the chopper brought. Sometimes, that got very interesting.

Hospital ward surrounded by sandbags.

Nurses tent and shower facility.

Latrine

Dr.s' tent and 19th hole (club tent)

Headquarters & mailroom

Chapel

Incoming Huey Helicopter

# CHAPTER 4

## Orientation Day on RR/ICU

The morning came early, as mornings do. I was up and ready for breakfast. Dressing is easy when the only choice is fatigues. Cleanup was easy also - splashes of water. I mentioned that we had no running water. We also had no hot water. It was a five - gallon jerry can and a basin. I used one of my hangers to hang my wet towel and wash cloth. Teeth got brushed outside. In the heat of the summer, this was okay, but the winters in Vietnam did get cold. Not the cold that comes from ice and snow. It was a damp cold that permeated everything.

I reported to the RR/ICU as scheduled at 0700 (7 a.m.). When I entered the unit, I saw a beehive of activity. The night crew was reporting off and the new crew organizing the day. There were about seven patients left in the unit. Two were intensive care, and five would be transferred to the wards. Except for the operating room tables, there were no wheeled gurneys for transporting patients. If the patient could not walk, they were carried on a litter. Carrying a 190-pound young man with a leg or body cast was a job best left to the corpsmen. If the patients needed extra attention and the ICU was not busy, the patients were kept longer because the wards were staffed by one corpsman on each ward to about twenty-five patients. One nurse supervised all of the wards.

One look around the unit said a lot. The RR/ICU was brightly lit by florescent lights on the ceiling. There were eighteen beds. Poles for IVs, suction machines, and tables stood between each bed. The beds were lighter and smaller in width than regular hospital beds and had thinner mattresses. They had a crank at the bottom to raise and lower the head, and one to raise and lower the knees. It took a strong arm to crank them. Luckily we were all young and had strong arms. There was the usual assortment of IV poles, blood pressure cuffs, stethoscopes, and stacks of universal Army light blue patient pajamas, some with snaps that would let you open a sleeve or a leg around a cast. There were stacks of linens and green Army blankets for the beds. One end of the ward had a curtained - off area for extra supplies. There were Oxygen tanks, boxes of syringes of several sizes, wound dressings of all sizes, tubing for any occasion: for nose and throat suctioning, and catheters for urinary drainage. There were several types of IV solution bottles, and several boxes of IV multi-dose bottles of penicillin. Almost every patient that had surgery received 20 million units of aqueous penicillin (20 MUAP). Extra suction machines were in the storage area also. There were two types commonly used: Gomco intermittent suctions and Wangenteens that were modified siphons for suction of the GI tract after abdominal surgery.

The nurse's work area was next to the curtain. It was no-frills, with a countertop work surface used for preparing medications and IVs. It also had a lockable cabinet that held all medications, including narcotics for pain. Except for a crash cart with emergency-type drugs, very few medications were needed or stocked because the patients, although wounded, were all young and in good physical health. We did not have to deal with diabetes, heart disease, HIV, cancer, or any other type of chronic illness. A metal chart rack was sitting against the wall full of metal charts, and a small metal desk sat next to it. The chart was started in triage and followed the patient through his hospital stay.

After an introduction to the RR/ICU, I wanted to know a little more about patient flow through the system so I knew more about what to expect. The flow went as follows: Patients were brought into triage, where a doctor assessed the condition and sorted them according to care needed. If a patient's wounds were such that he was not expected to survive with any available treatment, he was set aside and cared for with comfort measures, pain medication, blankets, and so forth. We had none of these that I knew about. Surgical patients were sent to the operating room in an order determined by the surgeons. Patients with acute medical or surgical conditions that were beyond our capability were taken by chopper to Third Field Hospital in Saigon with a doctor and a nurse aboard. Medical and psychiatric patients were sent to the wards for further care.

We had six operating room areas. Most of the patients entering triage were surgical: gun-shot wounds, traumatic amputations, punji stake stab injuries in legs or feet, and blast injuries to all parts of the body and head. The normal routine was to run two to three rooms with complicated, more serious cases that took hours, and the rest with the simpler cases that moved quickly. The thought was, you can always bump a simple case for a major one. If you have all rooms going with major cases, there was nowhere to go if someone with a life-threatening condition came in.

Punji stake wounds were simple but had major life-threatening consequences. A punji stake was a sharpened stick stuck into the ground, with the sharp side sticking up and coated with human feces. It was pointed toward the oncoming troops and hit just above boot level. When the soldier stepped forward, the stick deeply penetrated the skin and muscle, leaving E.-coli and other bad bacteria in the tissue. These guys needed debridement and antibiotics quickly.

Gun-shot wounds were always surprises. They took eclectic paths through the body, sometimes diverted by bones and sometimes clean. Medical people had to turn the patient over to find the full damage. Some of the slower rounds made little entry holes but large exit wounds. Chest and abdominal wounds from gunshot or blast injuries sometimes took hours to find and fix all the damage.

Patients spent time in the RR/ICU and were transferred to the wards when they were awake and stable. When they were ready to be discharged, a determination had to be made. Doctors could not do what civilian hospitals do - discharge them home, because home was half a world away. If the wounds were such that the patient could return to duty in less than two weeks, we kept them. Yes, they did want to go back, because they left buddies behind. If convalescence would take longer than two weeks, they were evacuated to the next level hospital, either an Evac hospital or third field, for convalescence and then returned to duty if healed. Or, depending on the injury, they were sent to Japan or to the medical treatment facility nearest their home in CONUS(Continental United States) The Air Force did all of the patient evacuation, except the unstable and critically ill. Those went by Army helicopter with a doctor and nurse in attendance. Today the Air Force has fully equipped flying ICUs. In Vietnam, they did not. Things like the altitude and changing air pressure were hard on unstable patients. Helicopters were more direct because they could land on the hospital compound and not rely on an air-strip then ground transportation.

The rest of the twelve hour day was spent learning how things worked. The charts did not house the nurses' working notes. They were in a cardex-type flip file that housed transcribed doctors' orders on the top flap and nurses' notes on the bottom flap. It was a very efficient system. A space for every patient in a file that could be carried around.

A twenty-four hour report for the chief nurse and hospital commander had to be done at the end of each shift. The report was to give the commander details about the patients we had, the number of patients through the RR/ICU. It showed the number of patients remaining and gave details on the sickest ones. The report was done on all of the wards also.

That was a lot of information to absorb in one day. The two ICU patients left in RR/ICU needed constant monitoring. One had chest and arm wounds, a chest tube to drainage, oxygen, and an IV. The other had abdominal wounds, an IV, and a nasogastric tube connected to a Wangensteen suction. Both had Foley catheters for monitoring urine output. The patients needed checking for tube drainage, IV drips, vital signs, and level of consciousness. Those were familiar tasks I could do in this foreign environment, So I went to work.

# CHAPTER 5

## Settling In

Time sometimes flew and sometimes crawled by. I was settling in. I got into the routine of things like laundry pick-up and pill day (Mondays were CP pill day for everyone), and became an old hand. Pill day had to be noted because the CP pills produced rather inconvenient diarrhea in most people, and the outhouses were busier. I got used to the distinctive sound of the rotor blades on a Huey (the chopper that brought most of our patients. It was the call for all hands to meet at the chopper pad. Even today, forty years later, I recognize the sound of the Huey, and my heart beats a little faster for a while.

While it was still warm, I used the community shower. It was in a rough, drafty building near the doctors' and nurses' tents. The door had a sign that read MEN on one side and WOMEN on the other. Just turn the sign according to who was in the shower. Using the shower required planning. There was a big water tank sitting on a structure next to and above the shower building with a ladder leaning against it. One had to climb the ladder and light the fire under the tank to get hot water. Nobody wanted to climb the ladder. If a nurse saw a doctor up on the ladder lighting the fire, a few nurses would run in and take possession of the room, turn the sign, and use all the hot water. It did not take the doctors long to figure that out and work in groups. I used the shower a few times when it was hot. It was bug-infested, as was everything else. When it got cold, I would not take off enough clothing to use the shower.

I was getting to know the people I worked with. The non-commissioned officers (NCOs) or corpsmen/medics were clinically outstanding and fonts of information. The ones I worked with most of the time were 91Cs, or 91 Charlies, an LVN equivalent in civilian life with more training. The wards were staffed by 91 Bravos, sort of a nursing assistant in civilian life but much better trained for being a field medic. Doctors and nurses were essential because of their extensive education, but it was the NCOs that kept the place running well. The senior NCO managed the unit. He kept the ward stocked with supplies and managed the corpsmen's schedules. The corpsmen were often pulled for other duties around the camp. In 1966, supply lines were not computerized. If we ran out of something because of a frequent supply line glitch or an upswing in use, the NCO would have whatever it was for us in hours. We never asked how.

"Other duties" consisted of company details that were needed to run the company. Things like errands, water pickup and delivery to fill the water buffalos and other places, guard duty, honey-pot duty, and so forth. "Honeypots" were the large metal half-barrels in the outhouses that caught the waste. They had to be pulled out and burned once a week. Nobody liked "honeypot" duty. The duty guy would knock on the door to let anybody inside know he was there and then walk around to the side, open the trap door, and pull the bucket out, replacing it with an empty one. Usually we knew when they were coming and waited. Occasionally his day would be brightened when he heard a screech from inside.

Every night we went to sleep to the sound of outgoing artillery fire - a loud boom and then a *whoosh*, and the sound of "Puff the magic dragon" - a Chinook helicopter with mini-guns mounted on the nose. The mini-guns sounded like a very large dragon breathing fire. By day, the Chinook was a workhorse; by night it protected the perimeter.

October moved into November without too much fanfare. It was getting cool, especially at night. I was able to acquire a wonderful, heavy regulation, army green pullover sweater. We had periods of quiet, so we could catch up with supplies and cleaning, around a steady flow of patients from minor skirmishes and injuries in base camp. The base camp was like a construction zone. The potential for injury was always there. We got people with broken bones and sprains. One man jumped off of the back of a deuce and a half (a two and a half-ton truck) and caught his wedding ring on something, pulling the skin off of his finger. It was called a degloving injury. He had to be sent to Saigon for treatment, probably skin grafting.

Gun-shot and punji stake wounds, traumatic amputations, and mine explosions were the bulk of our patients. The Viet Cong was very clever at stealing our trash and putting the shards of Coke bottles and the metal from the C-ration cans into mines. We knew that because the surgeons pulled the pieces out one by one. Every patient coming out of surgery got 20 million units of aqueous penicillin IV to avoid infection. The IV bottles were labeled "20

MUAP" so the next person would know it was added. The penicillin was in powder form and had to be mixed with saline and then added to the IV bottle.

We also had Vietnamese patients from a program called the Medical Civil Action Program (MEDCAP.) When we were not busy, teams of medical personnel went out into the villages and provided medical assistance to the villagers, often bringing them back for surgery on horrible, long-neglected tumors or for injuries like broken bones or deep cuts. The villagers welcomed us during the day. I would not have gone at night.

I saw Vietnamese workers on our compound. They built buildings, repaired the sand-bag bunkers around the hospital, and did other repair work to free up the soldiers for fighting. They were very pleasant, did not speak English, and happily did their jobs. They were starting to build something uphill on the other side of our utility road. I was mildly curious, but when you work twelve-hour days, fatigue usually beats curiosity, and I did not actually go look, always planning to later.

We got to know the helicopter pilots and a few people around the First Cav. base camp. Our headquarters would get calls inviting all the nurses to various parties around the camp. Of course, all the nurses could not go -someone had to work. We were a 24/7 operation. The parties were fun, but short. We danced to current music and talked about home and things we did not have and listened to war stories. When I heard a helicopter pilot talking about going somewhere (non-combat, of course) on my day off, I would ask to go.

My first trip was a supply run to Qui Nhon, a PX run for me. I took my camera everywhere. Qui Nhon was on the coast about a forty-five minute trip away over unfriendly territory. It was also the home of the sixty seventh Evac Hospital. The chopper, a Huey, flew ten feet off of the deck the whole way. If a tree was in the way, the chopper went up, over, and back down. The pilot told us he flew low so the Viet Cong would duck instead of shoot. I was scared but loved every minute of the ride. The PX was nice by war zone standards, not U.S. standards. It had a lot of stuff to buy. I was like a kid in a candy store looking and touching everything. I did not buy much, just stuff I needed, like camera film. Finished, I went back to the terminal and waited outside for a ride home. It was fascinating just watching the activity at the airport. Any change of view would have been fascinating after being buried in an ICU/RR twelve hours a day.

A week or so later, the second opportunity to ride somewhere was a resupply trip to the top of Hong Kong Mountain. This time, we were in a Chinook carrying a large bladder of water in a sling below the aircraft and boxes of food and fuel inside for the troops on top of the mountain. The view was great. I was very careful to stay out of the way while the men worked on the swinging water bladder. I saw neat rows of farmland and hills, all a lush green. Beautiful country.

In mid-November, the simple routine was over.

Helicopter ride to Qui Nhon

Old Shrine

giant Buddha

Chinook - Helicopter ride to top of Hong Kong mountain.

# CHAPTER 6

## My First "Push" (Mass Casualty)

The morning started out quiet. It was hot again; the air was warm and heavy with humidity. I struggled to pull my clothes on over damp, sticky skin. I first shook them out to make sure no bugs crawled in. I really hated bugs, but they were a way of life. I walked from our "hooch" to breakfast and then to the RR/ICU. As I stepped into the ward, I gasped with the first breath of air conditioning. It was a shock to lungs and sweaty skin. The night crew reported off and left. The two corpsmen and I had one ICU patient left from three days ago and several minor surgery patients left from yesterday. The corpsmen beat me to the unit and were already working. We had to move the minor surgery patients to the wards. The ICU patient would probably stay another day. He still had tubes and an IV. Then we had to restock and clean up for the next group of patients.

Lunchtime rolled around, and we took turns going to the mess hall to eat. Coming back from lunch, I stopped abruptly for a second. A cold chill ran down my spine as I felt, more than heard the distant *thrump, thrump, thrump* of Hueys coming our direction. I quickly ran back to the recovery room to alert my staff. All three of us went into automatic, checking supplies, restocking drawers, cleaning and remaking beds, and checking equipment to get ready for - what? We would not know the type and number of wounded until they got there. We had to be ready for anything, soldiers, prisoners, and Vietnamese civilians with any kind of injury or illness. The patients arrived in groups, muddy, dirty, and bloody, all blended with sweat. Most had been in the field for days or weeks and had not been near a hot shower.

As the choppers got closer, it was clear that two would be arriving soon. The Hueys were configured to carry a mixture of litter and ambulatory patients, up to thirteen at a time, depending on the mixture. It was obvious that nobody counted well because the choppers were usually jammed. Nobody was left behind. It was a wonder they got off of the ground.

When the first chopper landed, every available corpsman was there to help carry or support the wounded as they limped into triage. All the patients were quickly evaluated by doctors, and several were chosen to go to surgery first through a prep area. In the prep area, most of the dirt was washed off, at least near the injury. Remember that we did not have running water.

The operating room teams started arriving as the choppers landed. They quickly set up the rooms, evaluating by injury what they would need in the way of instruments. I don't know how they did that. They were very good at what they did. To start, four tables were set up to take care of minor injuries that could be dealt with quickly. Two rooms would be used for the major cases that took hours of operating time, like vascular injuries, and chest and abdominal injuries.

It was not long before the first patients began to move into recovery. The corpsmen and I started with the usual checks: airway, vital signs, level of consciousness, dressings, IV monitoring, limb circulation, checks of fingers and toes, casts. We watched for levels of pain, and I gave medication when needed. We fully expected that these men would wake up and move on to the wards to make room for more coming in. Time passed, our eighteen beds filled up, and nobody stirred. The corpsmen and I looked at each other, sighed, and started around again. There was no medical reason these men were not waking up. I walked up to one man who was laying on his left side with his arm extended out beyond the bed. He was on his side to keep his airway open because he had shrapnel wounds on his body and face, with dressings over his eyes. As I leaned down to check his dressing, my then-longer hair brushed his hand. I felt his fingers ruffling through my hair. I lifted up an eye patch, and his eye rolled in my direction and focused on my face. "Hey," he said in a loud voice. "A girl!" "From home!" One by one, around the room, the men said, "A girl?" "A girl?" "A girl?" They all woke up, sat up where possible, and looked. In a brief second, I realized just how much it meant to these men to see female nurses from home taking care of them. The corpsmen and I looked at each other and burst out laughing. We were working our tails off, and they were hiding. This was probably the first bed they had slept in for weeks. I said, "All right, you guys, you are out of here!" There was a chorus of groans. We moved them one at a time to the wards, and we just had time to clean and remake the beds before they were filled again.

Choppers kept arriving at spaced intervals for a couple of more hours. The injuries were from "booby traps," gun-shot wounds, traumatic amputations, broken bones, punji stakes, mine explosions, and shrapnel in all parts of the body. Shrapnel wounds covered a wide area but were generally shallow. They were painful, and it took a long time to pick all the pieces out.

It turned out to be a very long day, made easier by that incredibly light moment. We were on our feet working for at least twenty hours. More nurses and corpsmen came in to help as the more seriously injured, less stable patients came out of surgery. The mess sergeant brought food and coffee, and we took quick bathroom breaks. The focus was always on keeping these men alive and safe. With three exceptions that I know of, if a soldier made it to our hospital, he made it home.

Emotions run high during a "push," or mass casualty. I would run through the entire range of strong emotions in minutes. My heart went out to these guys. I remember one young man who came to recovery with a missing right arm below the elbow. I knew I would be there when he opened his eyes. What would be the first thing he asked? I was mentally preparing a response when he surprised me with: "How are my legs? I love to dance." I said, your legs are fine," and put him through a "wiggle your toes and bend your knees" routine. Satisfied, he went back to sleep. He already knew about his arm. Dealing with that would come later.

If I dwell on it now, some of the sights, sounds, and smells are still very real. They were perceived at the height of emotion and are etched forever in my mind. Tears are filling my eyes and cascading down my cheeks as I write this. That was forty-eight years ago, and it is as fresh as yesterday in my mind.

The chief nurse watched the flow of patients and sent staff where needed. This time she came to the three of us who had been working from the start and pushed us out the door under protest. I could not leave without reporting off to my replacement and charting one more thing. Luckily, I did brief "chart as you go" charting. The casualties had stopped coming, but the operating room was still busy. It was time for us to quit. I had been working on adrenalin and coffee for quite a while, and it was taking its toll. The cool morning air was welcome, but that was all I noticed. I went to my hooch, took off my boots, and stretched out on the bed. I could feel each muscle twitch as I started to relax.

I woke up several hours later. I got up and went back to recovery to help the crew that had been working while I slept. It would take days to finish up the work. The men on the wards would have to be discharged somewhere in the evacuation system when the doctor said they were ready to be moved. They had to make room for the new patients from ICU/RR. We had administrators on board who were experts at planning and arranging air transportation for patient evacuations.

As normalcy started to return, I had two things to look forward to. Thanksgiving was coming, and I had to do something with my hair. It was too long and hanging in my face. War zones did not have beauty shops.

# CHAPTER 7

## Haircut

My hair was brown, and so thick that it moved away from the scissors. It was cut short, with bangs covering my forehead. Sometimes I curled it, but for Vietnam, I just left it easy care - wash and wear. Now, it needed cutting. I could not procrastinate any longer. So, I started asking around about haircuts. I did not consider the post barber. I did not like what he did to the men's hair. I don't think he was a real barber. He was just the guy that got assigned to haircut duty that day.

Examining my options, I looked around the compound. The chief nurse had long hair that she tied up in a bun. Several of the other nurses did the same. I spoke with the nurses that had short hair; they were also looking for someone to cut it. Some of them cut their own hair a little at a time. See a long piece, cut it off. At work that day, I brushed the hair out of my eyes with an impatient swipe said loudly to no one in particular, "Does anybody know how to cut hair?" Several corpsmen and two patients volunteered, but I knew from the look in their eyes that they had mischief in mind and no real haircutting experience. I considered the Vietnamese workers, but they did not speak English. I did not know if they had our best interests in mind, anyway.

Finally, another nurse, Betty, and I sat down and thought about the situation. We rationalized that we should be able to solve this problem. Neither of us had any experience with hair-cutting, except maybe prepping a patient for surgery, and that did not count for much. That was shaving. We decided that we could cut each other's hair. After all, we watched as beauticians cut our hair, and my mother was a beautician. Some of her skills could have passed on to me.

I said to Betty, "I don't have any scissors. Do you?" We both had bandage scissors, but they were not sharp enough for hair. She shook her head no but offered to go to the operating room/CMS area to see if they had any surgical scissors that they were not using anymore. She came back later with a pair of general surgical scissors. We were ready.

I volunteered to be first. I sat down, wrapped a towel around my shoulders, and watched as the hair started falling. I gulped a few times, but said nothing. It would grow back, I thought. I started to be sorry that the hospital was a no-hat, no-salute zone. I may need a hat. When she finished, I looked in the mirror-face view only, and it did not look bad. I was pleased and felt much better.

Her turn, Betty sat down. She looked confident, but I did not feel confident. Her hair was blonde and fine, with a natural curl. I did not ask how she wanted it cut because all she was going to get was "shorter." I combed and cut, moved from side to side, lifted the hair like I saw the beauticians do, and cut. Hair fell in clumps like mine did, and when I was finished, it was a little crooked. I fixed that, and it did not look too bad. She very nicely said it looked great. We were okayfor a few more months.

As staff rotated home and new people arrived, we did get someone who knew how to cut hair, so we did not have to go through that again.

Time was getting harder and harder to track. Was it Tuesday or Saturday? The days were all the same; half was dark and half light. The patient flow was constant but not overwhelming. Some days were quiet enough to catch up with stocking and cleaning. I had a watch, so I knew what time it was, but hardly ever the date. The PX got a shipment of watches that kept track of the date in a little window on the watch face. I bought one and loved it. After a few months, I started to question its accuracy. I finally gave up. The day and date did not matter unless it was an important one. It was what it was.

# Chapter 8

## Visitors

Thanksgiving was a highlight. It came and went. We were treated to the traditional turkey dinner with all the trimmings. It was a little different on metal cafeteria trays, but those were normal now. We were entering the time of year with holidays. Visitors started coming. Martha Raye stayed with us when she was working with the First Air Cavalry Division. We did not see very much of her because she would be up early to go visit the troops in the field and come back late. She had a "room" in the nurses' tent.

The base camp of the First Air Cav was a big, busy place and centrally located, so we got a lot of visitors. I don't remember the order they arrived. I think Roy Rogers and Dale Evans were first. They were my childhood favorites, so I was thrilled to meet them. Other visitors were Bishop Fulton J. Sheen and Dolly Parton, and more that I don't remember now. The highlight was a visit from Bob Hope and the USO show.

Early in December, the rumor mill said that the USO show was coming to An Khe. This was a war zone, so flights were not advertised. A few days later, word came that the show would be arriving the next day. Somebody did a lot of planning; a partially covered stage magically appeared near the hospital. The next morning the doctors were quickly evaluating patients to see how many would be well enough to go to the show. Exceptions were the rule. The hospital had about fifty patients in some state of repair, with casts, bandages, open wounds, nasogastric tubes, and IVs, etc. When the time came, we gathered all the hospital personnel we could and disconnected IVs, carried, pushed, pulled, dragged, walked, and otherwise helped everybody that was not attached to the bed out to see the show. (Remember that we were on a rocky slope and had no wheeled chairs or litters except in the operating room - the tables had wheels.)

We grabbed blankets and pillows on the way. The weather was changing, but we hoped for the best. We got them all settled on the ground or propped as needed and patiently, expectantly, waited for the show to start. Doctors, nurses, and corpsmen sat near the sicker patients to watch for any problems. Luckily, nothing happened. With the troops from the cavalry, we had a huge crowd.

The show was fantastic from the first beat to the last bow. It was a touch of home, humor we could relate to, a light spot in an otherwise gray day. The men were totally mesmerized. Phyllis Diller was funny. The singers were wonderful, and Bob Hope was at his best. I look at the pictures now, and I cannot remember who the younger women were, but I bet the men remember. Midway through the show, it started raining, lightly at first and then in buckets. Water literally ran off of us. The show went on, and none of the men seemed to care about the rain. We covered the patients we could with blankets. I started to say something about wet casts and dressings, but they could not get any wetter, so we just watched the show and decided to repair the damage later.

When the show was over, Bob Hope toured the hospital to visit the men who were bed-bound. He walked down the wards shaking hands, saluting, waving, and telling jokes. I was part of the escort team. When we were partway down one ward, a nurse ran up with her camera and asked Bob if she could take his picture. He said yes and posed as only Bob Hope could pose - hand on hip, foot stuck out resting on heel, a silly grin, and a head tilt. She fiddled with the camera, and he posed again. It was a new camera. She fiddled again, and he posed again. Finally, with a twinkle in his eye, he looked at her and said, "Young lady, I don't pose this long for Paramount." Flustered, she almost dropped the camera. I don't know if she got a picture, I was afraid to ask.

After the brief hospital tour, the troupe loaded in jeeps and headed out for the air-strip and the next show. We waved as the jeeps passed by, very happy to have had the experience but sad to see them go.

Bob Hope lifted our spirits for a while. He was a great man.

I won't detail the hours it took to get everybody back in their beds, get IVs restarted, and clean up and dry out the damage from the rain. It did not matter. It was worth every minute. The show was the topic of conversation for weeks.

Christmas was coming soon.

Bob Hope show.

# CHAPTER 9

## Christmas

Christmas was just weeks away. The atmosphere in the hospital area changed. Many people, including me, longed to be home with family. We made the best of it. We found suitable but strange-looking small trees to decorate the wards and our hooch. The ornaments were whatever we could find. Empty C-ration can lids worked well. If cut just right into quarters just short of the center, the pieces curled so it looked like a pinwheel. Put a hole in one of the pinwheel blades and tie with a string to hang it and you have an ornament.

The hospital was quiet for a few days. We cleaned, repaired, and restocked. We did not have a radio that picked up very much. We could get Armed Forces Radio sometimes. If the guy with the radio held it just right on the right day and time and found the right station, we could pick up "Hanoi Hanna" and her anti-American rant. It was supposed to be scary but was usually funny.

More and more I was hearing stories from the injured men. The recurring story was that the soldier was approaching a village carefully and saw a child or a woman holding a weapon. The soldier hesitated for a second or two, and the child or woman shot him. He would say, "If I just had not hesitated, I would not have been shot, but that was a child."

The structure the Vietnamese workers were building on the hill was taking shape. We found out that it would be new female quarters - for nurses on one side and the Red Cross workers we called "Donut Dollys" on the other. We hardly ever saw them; they were always in the field with the troops. The building had six rooms on each side, with covered walkways and a real bathroom in the middle toward the back end, and a courtyard in between the buildings in front, a modified "H" shape.

The days moved on. I enjoyed the camaraderie in the Officers Club tent (the Nineteenth Hole). The way we worked, there was not much time to spend there. I did learn some dice games but usually lost to more experienced people. There had to be a trick to it.

I checked the mail room every day for letters, Christmas cards, and the boxes my mother sent with necessities. I asked her for "Cold Power" laundry detergent, light bulbs, and a few other things. All the lights in the hospital area were fluorescents; I could not get plain bulbs. I had a bedside lamp that needed a bulb. The box arrived, and I could not find the light bulbs. Thinking she forgot to send them, I said "Oh, well" and made a mental note to ask again next letter. I did some laundry the next day and found the light bulbs in the soap box. They travelled very well.

One day, I went to the mail room and had no mail. I turned to leave, and the mail clerk said "Wait a minute" and handed me an "any soldier" letter. I smiled and took it. I think he was feeling sorry for me. I took the letter back to my room and opened it. It had to have been a teacher assignment from an elementary school from the East Coast. I looked at it for a few days and then answered it. It was from a girl. I thanked her for the letter and told her who I was and what I did. I did not hear back. I still wonder today what her reaction might have been to that letter. Did she share it with her class?

The nightly serenade of outgoing artillery, the rotor blade roar and hiss of the Chinook mini-guns, was just background noise at this point. They were protection and appreciated for what they were. We had heard rumors of Viet Cong activity around the post, so I started sleeping in parts of my uniform, without boots and blouse but keeping a helmet close by.

Lulls didn't often last long. One afternoon we were mildly busy with cleanup chores and transferring the stable patients to the wards when we got a call that an emergency patient was coming by chopper a Vietnamese baby with croup. The now-familiar chill ran down my back. MASH units do not have croup tents or baby-sized anything. I looked at the NCO, and we said together, "Find ice." He ran to the mess hall, our only source of ice. I started gathering the IV solutions and emergency medications, dose unknown yet-this was a tiny person. Just then, the outer door at the end of the ward crashed open, with the medic from the helicopter moving quickly, carrying a very blue baby who was crying but making no noise. He was followed closely by the baby's frantic parents and one of our doctors.

The NCO was back with the ice, and I quickly turned the Gomco suction on and moved the tube from the suction outlet to the blow side so it would blow through the ice to create a fine mist. It worked, and the baby started pinking up. The doctor had gotten the IV started and was working on pediatric doses of medication needed to help the baby breathe easier.

The field equipment in our MASH was designed to work under primitive conditions. The old Gomco was a tried and true intermittent suction used for sucking out noses, throats, and airways in sick or injured patients. It was noisy. It sat on a small box on tall legs, with a catch jar sitting on a shelf between the four legs. It had a suction tube on one side and a blow tube on the other. The blow spout was a brisk exhaust to keep the motor cool. The Gomco was a workhorse, but not meant for continuous use. It got hot very quickly. I just hoped the infant would be better before the Gomco gave up. The baby improved with treatment, and the parents took him home twenty-four hours later. The staff in the RR/ICU took a while to calm down. We were very pleased that the baby did well.

A few days later, an NCO was going into An Khe, to shop for supplies. It was my day off, so I asked the chief nurse if I could go with him to Christmas shop.

# Chapter 10

## Trip to An Khe

The nurses, (all female,) on our compound were sort of a protected group. We were advised not to wander beyond the hospital area unescorted. Since the area surrounding the base was not secure, we were also advised not to leave the base without permission. In other words, don't go for a long walk to admire the countryside. The men could go anywhere the troops went. Every now and then the nurses could talk the hospital commander into letting us go off the base. This was just such a day. The hospital was quiet. We were given permission to go shopping in the near-by little village of An Khe. The company clerk was going into town on an errand, and we could go with him. We were excited; it would be a change of scenery after many weeks of hard work and sameness.

Early in the afternoon, the four of us (three nurses and one doctor), laughing and talking nonstop, piled into the jeep in front of headquarters dressed in fatigues, boots, and hats to wait for the company clerk. We had to trade our American money or script for Vietnamese money before we went. We only found out later that the clerk was delayed because he was checking to make sure the town was still secure. Details finished, off we went down the rutted, dirt road, bouncing up and down on the hard seats. We had to stop for herds of goats, swerve around mud puddles, and then slowly pass a line of young women in colorful *ao dais*, the local dress, as they gracefully walked somewhere carrying baskets of something green. We also passed the local contracted laundry. Clean American fatigues were hanging everywhere, on trees, fences, and some clotheslines. As we passed, the cloud of dust we created settled gently onto the wet fatigues, getting them dirty again. At least it was a change of dirt. The village was only a couple of miles away from our compound, but it took over forty minutes to get there.

As the jeep drove into town, the kids came running. We were mobbed with kids of all sizes looking for handouts, laughing and doing what kids do. They were used to soldiers driving into the village and knew they were good for candy and money. They did not get into the jeep, but they hung on the side. As soon as they saw the three of us, they quieted down and stared. They were used to seeing large American men. We were the first American women they had seen. And we were sized like the men - large. As small as I was, the Vietnamese women were shorter and smaller. One of the kids reached up and pinched me on the upper leg, I guess to see if I was real. That hurt. I yelled. Then the nurse on the other side got pinched. We hollered for help, the clerk speeded up a little, and the kids backed away.

We finally got to town. The main street (the only street, as I remember) was a dirt road. It had open, metal, patchedtogether, multicolored stalls lining each side. The street was about a block long. The stalls were selling a lot of daily living things for local residents, like food and clothing. They were also selling things Americans needed. Some of it was black market stuff that should have gone to the hospital. Theft is a problem in any war. It did not take the Vietnamese long to figure out we needed coat hangers, small dressers for clothing, and so forth.

We got out of the jeep and strolled from stall to stall bargaining for furniture, coat hangers, wood carvings, figurines, jewelry, and whatever else we could find. We had to be careful of the kids because they were still staring at us and would still land a pinch if we were not watching. We were not used to having to bargain prices, so that was difficult. It's a guilt versus value thing. This was an obviously depressed area to us, and the store-owners were great actors who spoke no English. We spoke no Vietnamese, either, other than simple words. We were targeted pushovers. Every now and then the company clerk would rescue us, but all in all, I am sure we didn't pay more than ten times the price we should have paid for any of the objects. Besides being bad at bargaining, we had to remember the value of Vietnamese money *(dong)* per dollar. At the time, it was thousands of dong per dollar. So if the guy wanted 300 dong for something, was that a good price? I didn't know.

Our shopping trip was well worth getting away for a change of scenery and an attitude adjustment. It was an education, a look into a small Vietnamese town to see how they lived and worked. That was the first and last trip the nurses made into town. It became unsafe for any American after that. It was okay with me; it took a while for the bruises to go away from being pinched. I still have and display the wood carving I bought.

Our trip home was uneventful. Home was starting to look good.

Dirt roads on trip to An Khe

Local laundry

An Khe local market

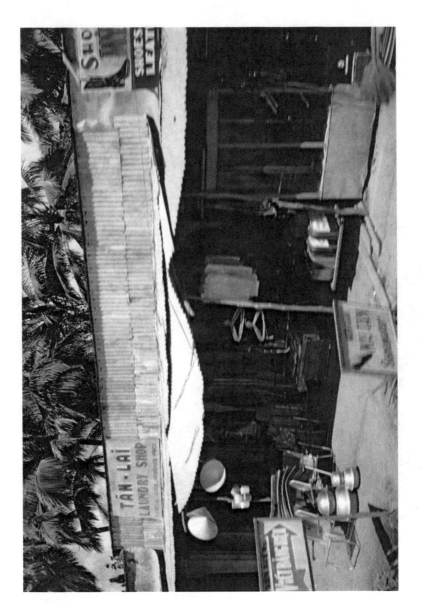

An Khe local market

Kids

Local Dress. We stopped to let them pass

# CHAPTER 11

## Daily Living

In an earlier chapter, I mentioned how people stared at us for being new when we arrived about four months ago. It was now my turn to stare. Our new chief nurse arrived. There are no words to describe how new she looked. Shiny new-car new. She was clean and bright, fresh in attitude, and full of energy. She had fatigues with creases in them. She was a major of average height and weight with dark, collar-length hair. I was starting to feel the effects of four months of work overload, inconvenience, and emotional rollercoaster rides. It was amazing what normal had become for me in just a few months. Her cheerfulness was definitely out of place in my world at the moment-needed, but more than a little annoying. I did not express that. I greeted her with a weary but sincere welcome. She would be my boss and needed to "learn the ropes" like everyone else. I would be helpful, courteous, and nice. After all, she was facing a whole bunch of people just like me.

She toured the hospital on day two to learn how things worked. She would offer suggestions for improvement. Most of the time I just had to tell her we had already tried that and it was not practical. She caught on quickly and started respecting us for what we were doing. Wise move; she got the support she needed. When she got acclimated and learned how things worked, she could and did make suggestions that were helpful. A new perspective is always welcome.

Christmas came with a small amount of enthusiasm. My packages from home arrived mostly intact. Home-made cookies never made it through the APO blender. They were good anyway. Mom sent necessities; I had no room for gifts. We had a big church service and a special Christmas meal of turkey and ham with biscuits, potatoes and gravy. It tasted good even on the metal mess hall trays. The patients were glad to get real food any time because they had C Rations in the field. The ambulatory patients all went to the mess hall to eat. It was Christmas in my heart and mind, and it was especially nice. The battlefields were also quiet. We had no new patients for several days.

We had one ward that was dedicated to Vietnamese patients when we had them. We had an interpreter available all the time. That ward had seven patients on it all recovering from some kind of surgery. When the patients were discharged, a MEDCAP team made follow-up visits to make sure they were healing properly. One of the teams was trusted enough in one village that parents approached them seeking treatment for their daughter. She was about twelve and had been locked in a closet for years because she was deformed. Her tongue had been growing for years. She could not close her mouth or talk very well anymore. It protruded several inches and was large in diameter. She had difficulty eating anything but liquids. The doctors brought her to our facility and did surgery to reduce the size of her tongue and try to correct her jaw so she could close it. It was marginally successful. Through an interpreter, they found out that she was mentally not right, probably from being scared, locked in the closet, and not being able to eat well or socialize.

One of our post op patients was a Montagyard man with a casted leg injury. We took a trip out to his village to make sure he was doing well. The homes in the village sat on stilts, with crude ladders for steps. He and his family welcomed us with smiles and thank-you's. He was healing well and still proudly wearing the light-blue Army-issue pajamas he went home in. I was curious about that because they were much too big for him. Normal attire in the village was a loin-cloth wrapped well. The pajamas must have been a badge of honor or something nobody else in the village had. I was pleased because he was happy.

All the Vietnamese patients we got had intestinal parasites in large numbers. Those had to be dealt with before surgery could be done. One Vietnamese soldier had a gunshot wound to the abdomen. He was bleeding and went to surgery quickly. They had to resect a length of bowel during surgery. We heard loud voices, a flurry of activity, and a door crashing open, coming from the operating room. That was unusual, so we went into the covered corridor outside the wards and found a couple of the OR staff members laughing and gagging. When the resected piece of bowel was put on the back table, a very large worm crawled out of it, contaminating the whole area. The nurse and scrub tech were not happy.

We toasted the New Year with a small celebration. The weather was cold in early January. The rain came down in buckets and sheets for days at a time and would pass, leaving mud and rivulets of water running down our hill. The sandbags around the wards kept them from getting wet. The cold penetrated everything. My new sweater became a necessity. The three of us were still in the Quonset hut protected from the weather. We had to walk through the mud and rain to go to work or eat. Everything I touched felt wet. People walked around in ponchos, giving the atmosphere a haunting gray look. The patients were coming in smaller numbers. I decided that it was time, people were telling me it was time, for me to go on my R & R(Rest and Recreation) trip. Everybody got one week to get away, and we had a choice of several places: Hong Kong, Singapore, Hawaii, Australia, and Thailand were among them. I thought Singapore would be great, but Hong Kong was available during the time I wanted. My orders were cut for a week in Hong Kong in four days. That would be time to get my civilian clothes ready.

These were arranged trips for group travel. The plane ticket was a set of orders; the hotel, chosen by an agent. The Army did not send weary soldiers off on their own to flounder in a foreign country. Once there, you could do what you wanted to do after a lecture on how to stay safe. Tours were available, also sanctioned by the Army.

Many of the married people flew to Hawaii to meet spouses on R-&-R. Nurses going to Hawaii made a list of things we needed and carried back bags of stuff from Tripler Army Medical Center in Honolulu. At the time, that was called a "petty-coat" supply channel. Computers have pretty much eliminated those channels. Too bad, they were effective and efficient. Nothing ever left the system. It just was not where it started out. We got a lot of things for patient care that the supply line did not have -but would have after we found out about them. Army nurses are a determined group.

Montagnard Village

Montagnard man

# CHAPTER 12

## Hong Kong

The thought of leaving in a few days to rest somewhere exciting gave me energy. I started looking at the civilian clothing I brought and thought it would have to do. I had slacks, a skirt, some blouses, and some walking-type shoes. When I packed to go to Vietnam for a year, I did not know what I would need. As I was packing for this trip, I thought of hot showers, a comfy bed in a well-lighted, decorated room where you could actually see out of a window. And I thought of restaurants and food served on plates followed with a lump of something good for dessert. I smiled.

The days passed quickly. When my departure day arrived, I got up early, picked up my orders, and signed out. The company clerk took me to the flight line. I boarded a C-130 on a routine flight south, and we landed safely at Can Ranh Bay. I checked in at the terminal and gave them a copy of my orders. My flight would be leaving in about an hour. This would be a full flight going to Hong Kong in a civilian chartered aircraft. I was getting excited and nervous.

The aircraft arrived, we boarded, and quickly left. The civilian pilots did not like to stay on the ground any longer than necessary. It was a nice flight to Hong Kong. As we circled waiting for our turn to land, I was able to look around and see the magnificent city. The runway jutted out into the middle of the bay. This was a busy harbor. It was crowded with cargo ships, small private boats, and harbor patrol boats. The city was hilly, spread out for miles on both sides of the bay. I could see tall buildings, streets, stores, and large homes on some of the hills. The plane landed and taxied toward the terminal. The guy in charge of the group stood up and started giving instructions about what we were to do when we entered the terminal. When we got through customs and picked up our bags, we were to report to a room at the airport for further instructions. We were all funneled together to baggage and customs.

With bag in hand, I was funneling into a large room with the guys. It was set up like a lecture hall. Before I got to the door, a hand reached out and pulled me out of line. He said, "You don't need to go in there." I gave him a strange look and he gave me a smile and a knowing look. It took a minute to realize that the information they were getting pertained to finding the safest brothels, and how to stay out of trouble and not disgrace the U.S. Army. I said "thank you" and he pointed me to the next step, transportation to the hotel.

The hotel was a high rise, not far from the airport. The van traveled through busy city streets with lots of turns, horns honking, and congestion. I checked in and was given a room on the eighth floor. I went to the elevator and, with a large smile on my face, pushed the button. The doors hummed open, and I got on. The doors hummed shut, the elevator quietly rose, and I got off on the eighth floor and walked down the hall to my room. I put the key in the lock and turned it. The door swung open on the most beautiful sight I had seen in months - a real bed with colorful bedspread and pillows, a bathroom, and a window. Through the window in my room, I could see some buildings, a few busy streets, and the bay. Between the buildings, I could see planes landing at the airport. I stood and stared out the window for a long time, just watching the beehive of activity. Civilization was a welcome sight. Then I sat on the brightly colored bed to see how soft it was. It was perfect. "Perfect" had a very broad definition at this point. The hotel had all the amenities that I had not seen for a while - running water, flushable toilet, sink to brush my teeth, and a mirror to put on makeup, which I also had not done for a while. I unpacked and shook out my clothing to hang up. What would I do for the rest of the day - absolutely nothing! Room service and sleep. I would see what there was to do tomorrow. I had a handful of brochures of things to do, but not today. I was going to enjoy a shower and crawl into that wonderful bed.

I slept a little later than usual the next day, had a room service breakfast, and then decided to start exploring. I took my hand full of brochures and headed for the concierge to plan my week. Dinner was a "welcome to Hong Kong" courtesy of the hotel that evening. The next few days would be tours of Hong Kong and the New Territories. They were British at the time, on a ninety-nine year lease. Today, they belong to China. The lease expired a few years ago. That done, I went outside and explored the area around the hotel. It did not seem smart to walk too far from the hotel until I knew the area better.

Dinner was near the hotel. The dimly lit restaurant had a small room on the side that a whole group of us were crowded into. There was just enough room for the big round table and about twelve chairs. On the table was a huge, tiered turntable, sort of like a huge lazy susan, where all the food would be served. When the food started coming, it did not quit. We casually ate for hours. The waiter kept filling the little dishes with more and different types of food. I only got a little of each thing before the lazy Susan would turn and a new treat would appear. I did learn to master chopsticks; that was all that was available. After a while, I had no idea what I was eating. It was just as well. I did not need to have an opinion, and it was all better than the B rations I was used to eating.

Tailors were very inexpensive in Hong Kong, so having an item of clothing handmade was almost mandatory. The tailor was on the list of things to do. I had a very nice suit with skirt and jacket made and ended up having them send it to my parents' house so I did not have to carry it back to Vietnam. When I got home, I had lost enough weight that it did not fit anymore.

The next day was the first tour. It was a tour to the New Territories. Hong Kong is an island, and the New Territories were part of the city but on the mainland connecting to China. We were in a twelve passenger van. We passed beautiful gardens, and a Sampan village that was out on the bay. People lived and worked on the Sampans. They would go out fishing for the day and come back to park eight or so deep from the shore into the bay. On the thirty-mile trip to the Chinese border, we saw more gardens, ate lunch at a nice restaurant, and stopped where the road ended-at the border of communist China. I took a lot of pictures. I met a lot of wonderful people on these tours. On this tour, I met a group of Australian soldiers on R-&-R. They were a lot of fun.

Hong Kong was a fascinating mixture of east and west. I felt full of courage one day, I swallowed hard, and hired a taxi to take me to areas of the city that the tours did not go. After haggling over the price, the driver agreed and off we went, winding through narrow streets, passing outdoor markets with large quotas of flies and hanging meats, down broad avenues and across tracks. We passed the grand communist China bank and department store, both with huge red Chinese symbols hanging in front. We went up hills where the affluent lived in huge mansions with a view of the bay. Then we cane back down again to see the British markets and central Hong Kong. When we got back to the hotel, I thanked him and paid him. When he left, I breathed a sigh of relief. It was a great tour, but I would not do that again. Some of those streets and places were frightening. I was glad the taxi did not break down or that I did not end up dead in an alley somewhere. I made a mental note to stick to guided tours in strange countries, especially when I am by myself.

The last tour included an afternoon Chinese play. The play was in a small, dimly lit, theater on a narrow back street. It was a story about Little Eva and Uncle Thomas. The costumes and makeup were lavish and scary. The drama, as acted, left no doubt in my mind what was going on.

The week went quickly, and it was time to leave. A van took us to the airport. I said goodbye to Hong Kong as I boarded the plane. We had an uneventful flight back to Cam Ranh Bay. I checked in at the terminal and took a seat preparing to wait awhile for a flight north. In less than an hour, the clerk at the desk motioned to me and said there was a helicopter heading north where I needed to go was I interested? I jumped up, and if the clerk had not been behind a counter, I would have hugged him. It couldn't get better than that. Hiding my enthusiasm, I said, "That would be great. Thank you." He directed me to the terminal exit and a helicopter standing by. The pilot was flying alone, so he told me to sit in the co-pilot seat. He said that he needed me to balance out the aircraft – but he said, "Don't touch anything." I assured him that was the farthest thing from my mind. He had me put the helmet onwith the radio on a channel so we could talk. After he did the flight check, he started the engine and we lifted off. He made a big swing out over the water and flew about a half a mile off the coast the whole way to Qui Nhon and then inland to An Khe. Part-way up the coast, the pilot said, "Look at the small puffs of smoke out there toward the shore," "Someone is shooting at us." I saw the small puffs very clearly. I understood why he was flying so far out.

I heard the radio chatter as we passed near Qui Nhon on our way to An Khe. The pilot flew high this time, above the range for small arms. I again heard the chatter as we approached the First Air Cav terminal. He radioed in that he had a returning nurse on board. We landed safely near the terminal, and I thanked the pilot, grabbed my bag, and got out. It did not take long for the company clerk to come and pick me up.

I was glad to be back home.

Hong Kong

# CHAPTER 13

## New Quarters

It's hard to believe, but I was glad to be back in this place I called home. After dinner, I unpacked my clothes and neatly hung up what I could. I had washed most of the underwear and civilian clothes I had worn while I still had running water in Hong Kong. The rest I just folded and put in the locker for another day. I had enough clothing for now. I did not have to be back to work until seven p.m. the next day, so I had time to relax.

People asked me about my trip-I told them about Hong Kong and how nice it was to be back in civilization. I looked at their tired faces and reality set in. My mood got outwardly dampened. Inside I was still happy. The going and coming of personnel at our unit was not celebrated and barely noticed. From other books I have read about Vietnam, that was true in many places. When I left, I knew people would have to work harder until I came back. I did the same for them. When I went home, I was grateful to be going home intact, but very sad to leave people behind to do what I knew was a very difficult job. That was just the way it was.

One of the things I did with my free time was go and look at our new lodgings I waited until the workers were gone and strolled up the hill. When I got to the concrete walkway, I was pleasantly surprised. This was a palace from what I had been living in for so many months. The rooms were good-sized, with more than enough room for a bed and locker. The outside walls were not solid. They were solid from the ground to about three feet up, and then they were screens covered by louvers (boards slanted down) for another four feet, and then solid again to the roof. Inside, the walls were solid to the ceiling level but did not reach the roof. There was no ceiling.

The building was kind of a squared "U" shape. There were six rooms on each side, with the bathroom connecting them at the end. The bathroom had a row of sinks with running water, flush toilets behind partial doors, and showers with ledges for soap and shampoo. I could hardly wait to move in.

The next day, I slept through breakfast and made it in time for lunch. I had to adjust for night duty. I relaxed, read, and caught up on letters home. I knew the hospital was busy, so I put on my fatigues and went in an hour early. I got a nice "Welcome back," and the usual "You actually came back!" that always created a laugh or a smart remark. After the day's transfers, there were six patients left in ICU/RR, all with major trauma to limbs or to body areas requiring a tube of some kind. One had a whole leg cast and needed to be monitored for circulation to his toes. A blood ooze was starting to color the cast just below the knee. His toes were warm, and he could still move them even though it was painful to do so.

It was amazing to me that the morale among the troops was good even though they had the injuries they had. None of them complained of anything but pain, and that was justifiable considering the extent of their injuries. Looking back, I am also amazed that we never had anyone detoxing from drugs in our hospital. According to the media, drugs were rampant in Vietnam. I did not see it.

The day staff reported off at a quarter to seven and left. Five minutes later, I was back into the adrenalin high. It was like I never left. I made rounds and checked in with every patient to see how they were doing. They were all new to me, so I had to get a baseline in my mind. You can tell a lot just by talking to the guys. Their main concerns may not be what you think they are. The corpsmen did the rounds of blood pressures, temperatures, pulses, wound checks, circulation checks, and neuro checks where needed. We reminded them or helped them to change positions to relieve pressure areas. I gave medication for pain when needed, and the evening progressed. I brought the charts up to date, signed off doctor's orders, and made up the IV solutions for each patient, including the 20 MUAP mentioned in a previous chapter. Occasionally, an IV would stop working or infiltrate, and I had to restart it. The night was flowing smoothly, but I did not say that or think it. That would be a set up for a problem - a hex.

Food and coffee came at about midnight. The coffee smelled good. About 0200 (2a.m.), one of the patients started making noise and getting agitated. It turned out that he was dreaming that he was back on the battlefield and did not have a medical problem. Others would wake up to talk for a few minutes, use the urinal, or request medication for pain.

About 0500, the corpsmen started making the last rounds for vital signs, cast checks, etc. I made sure the IVs were all okay and finished off the charts, noting anything of importance that happened during the shift. The new crew came in at 0630, and we reported off. It had been a busy but uneventful night.

As I left the ICU and walked up the covered walkway toward the mess hall for breakfast, I noticed that the air was crisp and clear, with a slight breeze. The breeze was bringing the smell of maple syrup, pancakes, and bacon. I was suddenly very hungry.

The pancakes were as good as they smelled. I finished breakfast and headed for bed. Snuggled deeply into the covers, I was gone for the day. First nights are harder because of the lack of sleep the day before.

Sometime around two, someone came in and told me I was assigned the end room in the new quarters and that we would be moving tomorrow. I mumbled "Okay" and fell back to sleep for a little longer. Forced to wake up by a hooch-mate moving around in the Quonset hut making noise, I got up and got dressed. Excitedly, she explained again about the new quarters and that we would be moving tomorrow after they finished moving the furniture into each room. "Furniture" was a loose term. We got a bed of normal height, instead of the hospital bed we currently had, and a regular locker that was a little bigger than the hospital one. It was all good. What I really missed was something people do not think about; a towel rack. In a hot, humid climate, towels do not dry well, especially when they are bunched up. I managed with coat hangers and eventually got a nail in the wall.

The next night came and went. It was less busy, the patients were improving, and we got no new ones. This was moving day. I moved my things in the morning and looked around. The bed had a frame for a mosquito net and a net to put on it. The Quonset hut was dark without a light on; this new hooch was much brighter. There were no windows, but the louvers allowed a breeze to flow through the room. I slept very well the rest of the day - light, bugs, and all. When I got up, I tried out our new bathroom facility. It all worked.

I worked a week on night duty and then switched back to day shift. We were starting to get fewer patients. As it turned out, we enjoyed this new facility for about two months. The war was moving north, and we would move with it, but not before we saw a little action of our own.

# CHAPTER 14

## Incoming

Though things flowed smoothly most of the time, we had our share of frustrating days. Today was one of those. It seemed like nothing was going right. We had a small but steady number of casualties - not the usual rush, but we were running out of supplies. The shelf with sheets was not refilled, the IV solutions were getting low, and we were down to two bottles of intravenous penicillin. Every injured patient used one bottle in his IV, how could we run out? The NCO was working on the problem. It was cool but muggy. The rain was pouring down outside, making everything damp and sticky inside. The air conditioner could not keep up with the humidity. Clothing stuck to staff and patients alike better than the tape did, making It hard to manage dressings. Bandages were damp, and the new ones out of the package became damp quickly. It was just a yucky day. Everybody was in a surly mood. Usually it was just one or two people that were surly. Today was different.

None of the Vietnamese civilian workers showed up for work.

The civilian hires did cleaning, repair of equipment, and so forth. The fatigues and sheets were laundered off post. (I never asked how such a large amount of laundry was done in a place without electricity.) I did see the fatigues and sheets hanging out to dry on wires in yards beside the road, collecting dust from passing vehicles. When it was humid, as it was today, they built fires to dry the laundry. My fatigues always smelled like smoke. That was just the way it was. American bases, where-ever they sit, whether in San Francisco, Germany, or Vietnam, hire civilian workers. All the bases have the same set-up. The base commander has a staff; that staff has an officer in charge of civilian affairs. A military base could be a self-sufficient operation, but it is nicer to get to know the community and create business for them, even in a war zone. At a post in the continental United States, the civilian liaison would bargain for electricity, water, trash pickup, and so forth. In a war zone, all of that is done internally. I mentioned before that the surgeons dug coke bottle pieces and other odd items out of soldiers'wounds. Where possible, the post uses civilian sources for food and workers to help the local economy, release soldiers to fight, and to get to know the local people to, hopefully, create an atmosphere of mutual trust.

It was very curious that none of the workers showed up for work that day.

This universally down day wore on unchecked. I got off work at seven that evening, and went past the mess hall to see if there were any left-overs because, I was still hungry. I ran into the XO (Executive Officer), also looking for a snack. I asked what was new in his shop. He said that the First Cavalry perimeter guard had noticed elephants wandering around outside the compound. He said that was not a good sign. The Viet Cong used elephants to carry their heavy artillery. He was going to alert the staff to be ready for a possible attack. That woke me up. It would be a perfect end to a dismal day.

I went to bed fully dressed, with my helmet beside my pillow, under the ever-present mosquito net. Mosquitos were the least of the problems, large, ugly bugs and lizards falling off of the ceiling were scarier. Every night we fell asleep to the sound of outgoing artillery - a *boom, whoosh* combination along with the"Puff the magic dragon hiss." We heard all the usual stuff this night, but during a lull we hard a new sound: *whoosh-boom, whoosh-boom*. I sat up banging my head on the mosquito net. My heart was pounding, and familiar chill ran down my back. Those were incoming rounds. We were under attack. I heard people shouting and running. One of the sergeants came by, pounding on doors in the female area, shouting, "Incoming fire! get under something!" I grabbed my helmet, rolled out of bed, mosquito net and all, and then rolled under the bed to wait for the shelling to stop. This night, the shelling scared me more than the bugs under the bed did.

When the shelling stopped, I untangled myself from the mosquito net and, since I was already dressed, I looked around to see if everyone in my area was okay. Then I hurried down to the central meeting area, where damage control was working to assess hospital damage and patient or staff injuries.

Luckily, the patients and staff were all okay. None of the shelling hit the hospital. None of it hit anything vital. The Viet Cong were very poor shots. They did tear up the base runways pretty badly. We had one immediate casualty -an

American contract worker with a possible heart attack. A few more casualties came later with minor wounds and other problems.

Bright and early the next day, the Vietnamese workers showed up for work again, smiling like nothing had happened. They were all fired. So much for a friendly interchange of ideas and cultures and helping the economy in a foreign land, not to mention mutual trust. I need to add here that the Vietnamese civilians who were not involved in the fighting just wanted to live a normal life. By day, they were friendly to us and helpful. At night, things changed. They had to accommodate the Viet Cong because they were brothers, uncles, and neighbors. That was a hard way to live. I am not excusing the behavior, but I do understand. They were our enemies, at least some of them, and I had to keep that in mind. You did not know who was who.

# Chapter 15

## Poor Me Party

In the new quarters, life was a little easier. A hot shower helps a lot. We had a consistent, but smaller influx of patients. The new patients plus the wound revisions of the previous ones, kept us busy. Day duty turned into night duty again. I went to my room one morning and noticed a bad smell that I did not recognize. I looked around and found nothing. The smell seemed to be coming from the outside. I went outside and saw that one of the Vietnamese workers up the hill had hung his lunch bag on a louver outside my room. (Yes, we had a small, select number of workers back.) He saw me looking at it and rushed over, chattering the whole way, to pick it up. I noticed his apprehension, smiled, and said "thank you." That never happened again. His lunch included nouc mam, the source of the odor.

Nouc mam was a Vietnamese fish sauce made of herring and sardines or other handy fish. The fish was placed in a two-tier crock on a rack and allowed to rot and drip into the bottom. They used what dripped down to create the fish sauce. I did not have the opportunity to try the sauce. To eat it, I would probably have to not know what I was eating, and it would have to have been disguised in something because it smelled terrible.

Day shift again. This was still winter, and the rain came and went, leaving us with puddles and rivulets running down the hill. It was a fact of life. We dealt with it. Bugs were everywhere. I shook out my clothes and shoes before putting them on - another fact of life. One day, I came home from work and one of the nurse anesthetists living in a room in the center had her door open. I heard a hissing noise. I looked in, and she had a can of heavy-duty Army bug spray in each hand, hands above her head, turning around and around, spraying until the cans were empty. We had no ceilings in the rooms, so the bug spray went the length of the building. I opened my door down the hall and found a bunch of dead bugs on the floor, and they were still falling with a *thud, thud*. She evidently hated bugs worse than I did. I stayed out until the bug spray dissipated a little. After clean-up, we were bug-free for a few days.

Tet, the celebration of the Lunar New Year in Vietnam, happened sometime in early February. It varied a little every year. It had been an occasion for an informal truce between the North and South Vietnam forces. This year was no different. That ended in 1968, with the big Tet Offensive that surprised everyone. This year was fairly quiet.

With today's mail came my *Time* magazine. I subscribed to *Time* to get news from home. The magazine was weekly, but through the APO blender, I got them in batches - a few at a time. It was not comforting to see all the reports about the anti-war protestors, the riots in colleges, and so forth. I tried not to think about it. One of the magazines had a story about Vietnam. As I read the story about how a base was attacked and had a lot of casualties, I began to feel sorry for the people on the base. I read all the way to the bottom of the page, hoping for more information. The line at the bottom gave the reporter's name and that he was reporting directly from the action in An Khe. I was confused. I was in An Khe, and we not only had no action, but we had no casualties that day. I put the magazine down and decided to think about the story for a while. I later found out that many of the reporters wrote their stories from a hotel in Saigon. That was changed for the Middle East wars. Troops now have reporters embedded in their units.

I had up and down days in Vietnam, like everywhere else. It had been raining too long. This was a "I have been working too hard, nobody appreciates me, I want to go home, and so what if I go AWOL, what are they going to do, send me to Vietnam?"- type day. It was silly, of course, and not even rational, but there it was. It was the bottom of the emotional roller coaster. We had fewer patients, so I had time to think and to dwell on the downside of my situation. It must have been in the air because two other nurses felt the same. We decided to have a "poor me" party. One nurse had a half bottle of vodka and a blender, and I had packages of Kool Aid. The other nurse offered her room and snuck into the mess hall for ice and some ugly, plastic, drinking glasses. We had a choice of Jolly-Ollie Orange or Goofy Grape blended with vodka. Firing up the blender, we had a grand time, laughing, telling stories, and generally airing our complaints. About an hour into our party, we heard a timid knock on the door. There stood a young mess cook with a tray of food. The mess sergeant was concerned about us. Surprised, we thanked him and closed the door. As soon as he was safely away, we burst out laughing. We could not get away from the fact that we lived in a small town and just could not get by with anything. I felt measurably better. Laughter is a good thing. The food was pretty good, too.

I perked up after that. My sense of humor and perspective returned. I realized that I was on the downside of my tour, I had been here for over six months, and the rest would be a breeze.

In a couple of days, I got promoted to Captain at a small ceremony in the Commander's office. I wore the shiny new rank proudly. I found some subdued brass at the PX and I was official.

# CHAPTER 16

## The Move

The hospital saw moderate activity for a few weeks. Winter turned to spring. We had a steady but small flow of patients with minor and major injuries. I was starting to find a routine, enjoy my new room, and otherwise relax. Big mistake. Mid-April, Second Surg was put on a seventy-two hour alert to pack up and move. We were going to Chu Lai, on the north coast, to support the newly forming American Division. We had to discharge or transfer all of our patients (about thirty of them) and pack our belongings, pack up the hospital, and leave. We had to be functional in An Khe to functional in Chu Lai very quickly not a small task. That familiar chill ran down my back again. Instant terror was getting easier to manage.

Second Surg started as a hospital in a box. It was called a Table of Organizational Elements(TOE) unit. It has a proud history dating back to 1943. It saw service in the South Pacific during WWII, in Korea, and now Vietnam. After Vietnam, it went home to Fort Bragg, North Carolina, to be boxed up again to wait for further orders. When not in use, it would sit on Fort Bragg staffed with an administrator, a chief nurse, and a complement of enlisted medics to keep it up-dated and functional. It would be mobilized at least once a year for a training exercise (FTX) to make sure everything worked. Then it was boxed again for storage. The training exercise many times was in conjunction with another unit FTX that needed medical "stand-by" assistance. This is the kind of hospital mobilized for disaster relief around the world.

Because it was a boxed hospital, it had a plan to set up and tear down quickly. A large computer printout listed everything the hospital was supposed to have, from tents and operating room tables to Q-tips and nurses, by specialty. We did not always use the standard items because the supply line kept us supplied with better stuff. For instance, the regular stock listed glass syringes and reusable needles that needed to be cleaned and sterilized after use. The supply line kept us stocked with disposable syringes and needles. Much better, but in a war zone, supply lines are not always reliable. You had to have a consistent source of supplies.

As a junior officer, my job was to take care of the patients until they were gone and to help pack up the ICU. I also had to pack my own things. That wasn't hard - I had not collected very much, but how I had collected anything was a mystery. The administrators very efficiently handled the formal move - the packing, the tear-down and set-up at our destination, and co-ordinating transportation. We could not travel by land because of the terrain, lack of roads, and enemy action. The hospital itself when boxed up would be travelling by flying crane. This was a huge helicopter with a cockpit connected to a tail with nothing in between until the container pods were attached.

Moving day came quickly. We were up in the morning dressed in full battle gear: helmet, web belt (no pistol), canteen attached, and dog tags. We were a sight standing by the bus waiting to board. Personal effects were on the bus already. One of the men had adopted a Vietnamese dog that became a company pet. He came along also. We boarded the bus that took us to the waiting C-130 and then quickly boarded the plane. The inside of the airplane was configured with canvas seats along both bulkheads, so we all sat facing into the aircraft. The middle was filled with cargo. I took a seat about in the middle and strapped in. The person holding the very calm and friendly dog was at the tail end of the plane. Before long, the plane was taxiing down the short runway and lifted off smoothly. We headed west to go north. I took one last look at my old home and said good-bye with a little sadness. I had left a piece of myself there. The green landscape passed by below. It was broken up by a clearing here and a village there.

About fifteen minutes into the flight, something scared the dog. He slipped out of his handler's grip, and in a panic, he raced around the airplane, hitting laps and boxes. People with flailing arms tried unsuccessfully to catch him because you can only reach so far when belted into a seat. Second trip around, he landed all four feet in my lap for a second, and I grabbed and held onto him until he quieted down. That shocked everyone awake for a few minutes.

The rest of the flight was uneventful. The plane was too noisy for conversation, and if the rest of the people were like me, they were trying not to think too hard about what was coming. It would get there soon enough.

We had been flying for about an hour when the pilot announced that we would be landing soon. I looked out the window and saw a large number of one-story buildings in rows, the ocean, and the beach. I felt better about the move already. This turned out to be an upgrade. I later found out that we were on a Navy base.

dressed for the move.

Helicopter Crane

Crane Pods

# CHAPTER 17

## Chu Lai

Our base in Chu Lai was very different from the one in An Khe. It was larger, more open, and more spread out. The ocean and the beach made the place seem like a resort. That was far from true. We were warned that the beach was not safe because the Viet Cong would show up every now and then. It was still lovely to look at. On the sand near the beach was our chapel, which looked like a large grass hut with a cross over the door sticking up to become a silhouette against the sky. Our outdoor movie theater had a large screen, several benches, and a lot of sand to sit on. The fresh air and cool breezes were wonderful.

We arrived, were shown our new living quarters, and found the necessities -latrines, mess hall, and headquarters. We would get a grand tour tomorrow. The hospital equipment was being placed in a prearranged set-up. Someone scouted ahead and decided what would be the best flow of patients given the arrangement of the pre-existing buildings. It was a given that if you were not part of the plan, please don't get in the way. My turn to work would come soon enough. I got myself settled and, curious, went to find the ICU/RR area.

The triage/ER area, the operating room, the ICU/RR and the Central Material Service (CMS) were grouped together in one area, and all were air-conditioned. All were in Quonset-type huts. The wards were in wooden buildings down toward the beach. The buildings did not have solid walls, but instead had screens covering the middle third of the wall space no louvers. That allowed for ventilation but not much privacy. The back of the wards looked toward the ocean.

As before, the staff lived around the hospital. The nurses' hooches were in a line perpendicular to and closest to the RR/ICU area. Men were quickly building a shower room, and a latrine behind the hooches and down a small hill. They later built a sand-bagged bunker just outside our back doors.

The hooches were actually small, bare, stand alone houses with front doors and back doors. No windows. They did not have solid walls. As before, they had screens and louvers. A living room in the front of each was furnished with a couch, a couple of chairs, and tables. In the back was a bedroom furnished with, in our case, three twin beds, two on one side, one on the other. The beds had mosquito nets, again for the lizards and large bugs as much as the mosquitos.

Our first night there, since our showers were not finished, the Navy officers very graciously invited the nurses over to use their showers. Five of us piled into a vehicle. We were dressed in fatigue pants, flip-flops for shoes, and Army green T-shirts, arms loaded down with towels, washcloths, and shampoo bottles of all colors. We arrived, and the guys came out to meet us. The showers were inside the individual hooches, two men to a hooch. Three of us were led into one particular hooch. The bedroom was wall-to-wall exercise equipment. One of the men living here was Roger Staubach, future pro -football player. He said hello, chatted a minute, and left. His hoochmate stayed to entertain us. He had a well-stocked bar, told stories and refilled our drinks as we took turns showering. That was a memorable evening, a welcome to Chu Lai. We were taken back to our area, clean, slightly tipsy, and very cheerful.

The next day, we were up before dawn. This would be a busy day. I went to breakfast at the mess hall, which was down toward the beach. This was an open-air mess hall. It was a covered building with grass on the roof, but it had a back wall and two side walls. The front was a half wall. It looked like a bar in a tropical island movie, just bigger. No doors. We were back to warm weather again. It was soon going to be hot and sticky. Breakfast was C-rations at first because they were not fully set up yet. C-rations were designed for maximum calories, so a little would go a long way. Flavor may have been an after-thought. Some were not bad. They all seemed to be high in fat. I liked the eggs and chopped ham; the high fat was natural. Groans from the troops were ignored. We ate quickly and reported to the chief nurse for duty assignments. I was still assigned to the ICU/RR area, so that's where I went. All the equipment was there; it just had to be arranged a little better - a "nurse arrangement" -and things put away. That took most of the day. We worked frantically because we had a time constraint. Patients would be coming soon. One nurse was sent home to come back later for the night shift.

We had all the same things we had at An Khe: the hospital beds and other equipment, suctions, catheters, all came from the packed boxes. There was one new item, a Foster bed. This bed was designed for patients with spinal cord injuries. It was a narrow bed on a frame. The patient would lie facedown with his face in a mask-type apparatus so he could breathe. When it was time to turn him over to protect his skin, the top of the bed would be fastened securely to the top of the frame, sandwiching the patient in. A belt circled the whole apparatus as additional security, and the whole frame would be rotated so the top would become the bottom and the patient would be lying on his back. The up-side of the frame would then be removed and the patient belted in again. It worked well. We used this bed one time, that I know about.

This was a larger hospital. The ICU/RR was a bigger area but had about the same number of beds. There were more wards for convalescing patients. Instead of three, we now had seven, with room for prisoners. Each ward held slightly fewer patients.

Triage was larger too. It had much more room to work and safely hold patients. We also had wheeled stretchers to move patients from one place to the next. The men no longer had to lift and carry the heavy, casted patients. It was a good thing because the distance was farther from the ICU to the wards. As in An Khe, the men who could walk, were walked to their new wards.

I left work at 7 p.m. as the night crew had arrived. We still had no patients, but there was work to do with supplies and equipment to get ready for the influx when it came. It would be coming soon. I went to my hooch, read awhile, and went to sleep.

A few patients arrived just before dawn. The helicopters were not as loud in Chu Lai, but I could still hear them. They may as well have been alarm clocks. I was instantly awake and alert, my heart racing as I automatically got up and dressed. That's what is nice about wearing the same thing every day-you don't have to think about what to put on. I heard many more people up, talking, and hurrying to get dressed.

Chu Lai Hospital & South China Sea

Lorna Griess

Wards

My shared "Hooch."

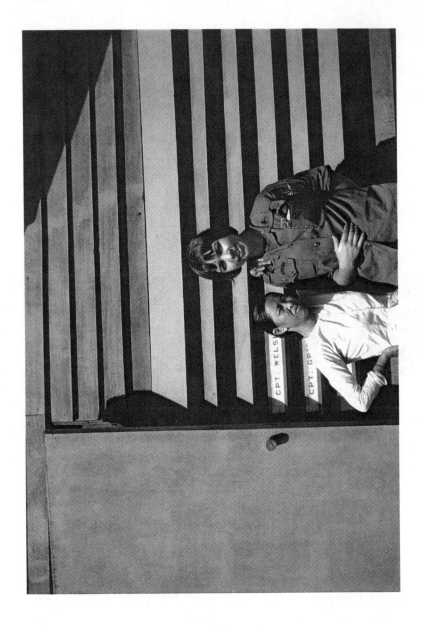

Cleaning Lady

Chapel

Lorna Griess

Movie Screen

# CHAPTER 18

## First Work Day in Chu Lai

Dressed, I ran to the ICU to see if they needed help. The patients were still in triage, so I went over there to check. There were six patients, some with GSWs (gun-shot wounds), some with injuries from exploding mines. They did not need help, so I went to have breakfast. I knew it might be too busy to eat later. The mess hall was all set up, and we were back to the good stuff - B rations. I had a surprise after I ate; the mess hall had some new rules that applied to everyone. When I was finished eating, I had to do my own dishes: scrape the tray, dunk it in hot soapy water, then in hot rinse water, and stack it on a rack to dry. If you do it wrong, you do it over. The utensils went into a hot soapy bin. I did not comment on any of this - I just did it. Easier that way.

After a stop back home to brush my teeth, it was about 0630, time to go to work. The night staff reported off. They had no patients but showed me where they put all the supplies. They did a good job, It was all arranged nicely for greatest efficiency, but this was going to take some adjustment. For months I was used to reaching in the same place for something I needed, and it was going to be somewhere else now. It only took a couple of days to get used to the new arrangement, though. It was better than what we had before. We had drinkable, running water. It made patient care much easier. We still did not have telephones on the wards, just the Army crank type that nobody could work. It did not matter anyway because anybody I would need to call from the ward, like a doctor or a ward to transfer a patient, did not have a phone to answer the call. That's just the way it was.

Before long the patients started arriving, one or two at a time. All had IVs, one had a nasogastric tube and an abdominal dressing, another had a cast on his leg, and the rest had bandages here and there. All did well. We were back to vital signs every fifteen minutes, cast checks, tube checks, and neuro checks for orientation and level of consciousness. I gave out medications for pain and did all the documentation. Everything went smoothly in our new ward thanks to the night staff for all their work organizing.

We got a few more patients throughout the day, most with extremity wounds. About half went to the wards the next day.

The days passed, and the work continued at a steady pace.

The hospital had Vietnamese workers who painted buildings, did maintenance on sand-bags, cleaned up around the compound, and so forth. Each hooch paid a Vietnamese worker, a woman in our case, to clean the hooch and do personal laundry. That worked out well. We got to know them, and they got to know us. The Vietnamese women and men were much smaller than we were. The cleaning lady in our hooch came up to my shoulder and was much smaller around. One day, the air conditioner in the ICU/RR quit working. They must have sent for maintenance. I was not at work yet. I was sitting outside my hooch and saw a Vietnamese man walking with a swagger toward ICU, dwarfed by his tool belt, to fix the AC. I was skeptical, in an area that did not have electricity in homes, never mind air conditioners, how was he going to fix the AC, but when I went to work later, the AC was humming nicely. He fixed it.

The area housing us women had a guard that watched the area 24/7. That was new. We had not had any trouble, but someone must have thought we needed one. There he was. He did come in handy on two occasions, which I will go into later.

I looked at what I needed in my hooch and decided I needed one of those small chests of drawers I saw at the market in An Khe. I looked for the company clerk to see if anybody went into the town here in Chu Lai on errands so they could pick one up for me. I knew I would not be able to go anytime soon, if ever. A few days passed, and the company clerk appeared with a small chest of drawers for me. I paid him the going price, very pleased with my new "furniture."

The chest was made of thin wood. The way it was made, it could not have been in common use in Vietnamese households. It had holes where the boards did not meet. It was a little higher than the bed, so it served as a bedside table. It was twelve inches deep and had four drawers that were only eight inches deep, leaving a big space between the drawers and the back of the chest. They were enough for what I needed, I filled them up with underwear and other clothing, books, paper, and so forth. I was happy to be organized. As I remember, the wood was covered with paper with a small flower design. It was sort of pretty.

Very soon our shower facility and latrine were finished and workable. Amazing how the definition of luxury changes with circumstances.

Americans did not work alone in South Vietnam. We had help from the Australians and the South Koreans. The South Korean (ROK) troops were tough, seasoned fighting men. When we started getting wounded prisoners in the hospital, they were mostly Vietnamese. We never knew much about them. We did get one North Korean prisoner. North Korea must have been helping the other side.

# CHAPTER 19

## You Just Have to Explain It Right

I woke up one afternoon in the heat and humidity. I had worked the night shift in ICU as usual. The night was fairly busy with patients left from action a day or two past. Choppers started arriving just after first light. The Army was engaging the enemy and taking casualties north-east of the hospital. Our shift got the first of the patients out of the operating room before the day crew arrived. The choppers woke up the entire camp, so people started arriving early.

When the day crew arrived, I gave them a quick report, and then we all spent another hour moving the recovered patients out to the wards to make room for more patients from surgery. I also had to finish up some charting on the patients remaining. That finished, the corpsmen and I said good-bye and went outside to a day that was cool but humid. This would be another hot day. I had just enough energy to eat breakfast before going to bed. My body was aching to lay down - anywhere. I slept soundly until someone made some noise outside my hooch around one o'clock, then off and on for the rest of the afternoon. It got hot. A gentle breeze blew through the hooch, but not enough to cool it down. I later managed to get a fan for the super hot days.

Groggy but up in the late afternoon, I read a little and then gathered my towel and wash-cloth from the nails on the wall and headed for the shower. Most of the day gone now, I headed for the mess hall for dinner and another night of work. When I got to the ICU, the operating room crews were just finishing with the last of the long cases. The ICU/RR was full, and the corpsmen were transferring stable patients to receive the last of the new ones. The day crew gave report, finished up, and left as the last patient came out of the operating room. Three Vietnamese prisoners were in the back of the ward with a guard standing by. All of the prisoners had extremity wounds and were restrained. The restraints were questionable because they were made for large American men. The Vietnamese were about half the size, so their arms easily slipped in and out of the leather wrist restraints.

Our newest patient was a North Korean soldier. He was still asleep. He had abdominal wounds with a large dressing and a nasogastric tube. He was a young man, small in stature but very muscular and still under anesthesia. We had him on his back, with a nasogastric (NG) tube taped in place and in four point restraints (all extremities). We pulled the restraints as tight as we could, but there was still wiggle room. The N/G tube needs to stay in place after abdominal surgery for a few days until the stomach and intestines are working again. Without it, the patient will be in pain or may need to return to surgery for a damaged suture line. Our soldier was sleeping nicely, vital signs were good, and the guard was watching while we cared for many other patients.

Our routine was still vital sign checks, sensory check, and a dressing check every fifteen minutes on all patients. Our prisoners were no exception. After the third check, he started to move a little. When I was several patients away, he woke up. He must have looked at his circumstances and did not like what he saw. He wiggled his right hand out of the restraint and pulled his N/G tube out.

The guard frantically called me back to see our patient. I looked at him and calmly explained in my best nurse English, using gestures, the importance of the N/G tube to his safety and recovery as I reinserted the tube and put his arm back in the restraint. He did not understand a word I said. I spoke no Korean, and he spoke no English. I sent someone for the interpreter assigned to the hospital, but he was out somewhere. No one knew when he was coming back.

I got halfway down the ward before the guard signaled me again. The patient had wiggled out of his restraints and pulled out his N/G tube again. This time he was looking at me with a proud, "I don't want this tube" look. I came back and spoke in harsher terms, shaking my finger at his nose, making gestures about an exploding abdomen and reinserted the tube and did not bother with the useless restraints. I hoped I had made my point about the tube. He was glaring at me. I glared back. I turned to go back to taking care of some seriously injured GIs, looked back at him, and saw he had pulled the tube out for the third time, glaring straight at me defiantly. I was done. I did not have time for this. The rest of the story is like a cartoon. Please don't do this at home. To this day, I don't know why I did it, Probably fatigue and total frustration. I put my hands up like a charging mamma grizzly and growled as

I ran back to his bed. He lifted his head, took one look at me, and his eyes got huge. He it out a sharp *huhhk*, picked up the N/G tube, shoved it back into his nose, and had it all the way down before I got to his bed. I checked his stomach with a stethoscope and a small injection of air to make sure it was in the right place, nodded my head, smiled, and said "thank you." He nodded in return. I did give him a shot for pain, which he probably needed by now. I had no further problems with him. In fact, I had no problems with anybody that night. I had amazing co-operation from everyone. See, you just have to explain it right.

I got off work at 7a.m. Free for a day, I went back to work the following morning on the day shift. The MD had just finished examining our prisoner and pulled out the N/G tube. When the MD left, the prisoner saw me, his eyes got huge again, he let out a sharp *huhhk*, and he started to panic. I just smiled and briefly bobbed my head, and he relaxed.

After a while, having Vietnamese prisoners was not unusual. The North Korean was unusual. Prisoners were considered valuable sources of information and were treated well. They were never a problem. Most of the prisoners liked us and the food, once they got used to it. Taking that first bite of food took a lot of trust and sometimes several missed meals. One of the prisoners was on his second day without eating, and I was there when a breakfast tray was put in front of him. Again he refused to eat. I said okay, took a piece of bacon off of his tray, and ate it as I left the ward. His eyes followed me out the door. He started picking at the food to see how it tasted. Then he cleaned up every tray of food after that.

# CHAPTER 20

## The Guard and More

After a couple of months of work in the ICU/RR, the chief nurse decided that we should share the load and rotate out of ICU and work supervising the wards. At first, I was a little disappointed. I had honed my skills and was proud of what I did. On the other hand, I was getting weary. I had worked ICU/RR twelve hours a day and six days a week for nine months. It was long past time to move, especially after we lost a patient from unusual circumstances, probably a pulmonary embolus. It was unavoidable but heartbreaking.

I was devastated. The ICU/RR was moderately busy this day, the beds were filled, everyone was doing well, and all were uncomplicated surgeries. One young man had a cast on his leg, his vital signs were good, and he was awake, talking to his buddy in the next bed. The next minute he had a strange look on his face and gasped he was gone. The MD and I started CPR, used all the right drugs, and worked on him for a long time, without any response at all. The MD thought it was probably a pulmonary embolus. With our limited lab services, there was no way to tell. We were all shaken. This was incomprehensible. We should not have lost that young man.

When a patient dies in a combat zone hospital, the mortuary services are called Graves Registration. We gently cleaned him up. The men from Graves came and got him. I never knew the location of Graves Registration at An Khe or Chu Lai. I never wanted to know. That is a tough job.

Did the staff get sick in a combat zone? Of course. Did we call in sick? No. We worked anyway. Several days I felt really bad, but better once I got to work. Once the adrenalin gets going, other things disappear. One day a surgeon came into the ICU, pale and looking pretty ragged. He started an IV on himself, ran in a liter of Lactated Ringers solution, and perked up enough to go to work. That is how we survived and did our jobs. One day at a time.

One day a nurse did get sick with vomiting and diarrhea that would not respond to the usual treatment. She was admitted to the only place a female *could* be admitted to the ICU. She received IV hydration for two days and was discharged to her quarters a few steps from the ICU. The nurses kept an eye on her until she was well enough to work.

Our cleaning ladies were working out well. After breakfast one day, I lingered a little longer talking to someone and I got home a little later than usual. Our lady had finished cleaning the hooch. I was about to get undressed and go to bed when I heard a knock on the door; it was the guard. He said, you may want to go down and check the shower. I hear a lot of giggling coming from there." Curious, I walked down the hill. Sure enough, there was a lot of laughter coming from the shower. I looked in, and the ladies were all together, ready to wash our clothes, but they were trying them on first. The bras wrapped around them twice. They saw me looking in and were taken aback for a second. I smiled and left. Humor is a good thing. I was just as amazed at their tiny sizes as they were at my large size.

Another guard story: I came home from work one day, opened the top drawer of my prized dresser, and almost vomited. There was a nest of four newly born baby *somethings* curled up in there. Everything in the drawer had to be tossed. I called the guard and asked if he would get rid of what-ever it was. He thought they were rats. Evidently, a pregnant momma rat crawled up the space between the drawer and the back of the chest and found what she thought was a safe place to have babies. I did not appreciate that. The guard threw them out on the ground in the bushes. My hoochmate saw one of them and brought it back in, thinking the dog had aborted. When I told her what it was, she turned a little green and put it back outside. The magic was gone from my dresser.

We had movies on the beach most nights, if it did not rain and depending on the supply line. In 1967, CDs and DVDs did not exist. I think they were movies on a reel that required a noisy projector. It was great, sitting on the beach in the open air watching a movie. They were movies from the '40s and '50s, the old standards. Most were guy flicks - war and action-packed stuff. It was all okay with me. When I transferred to work on the wards, I got to see most of them.

That evening we even had a company party. One of the NCOs, it must have been the mess sergeant, "found" a box of steaks somewhere. Instead of dinner one evening, we had a company party with a barbeque and all the good stuff to go with it. The party was more or less on the beach. The steaks were delicious, and we had a good time.

One morning in mid-summer, I was talking to one of the helicopter pilots. He said he was going to make a run to an island just off of the coast to deliver a three quarter-ton vehicle, and would I like to ride along? I would for sure. I checked with the chief nurse. Since I would not be on duty until later, I could go. Another nurse wanted to come along also. The pilot picked up the vehicle, and we headed out over the water to an island about a mile out. This island was rumored to be a Viet Cong R-&-R haven, but nobody was there today. We dropped off the vehicle and started back to the main-land. The pilot flew very low on the return trip. When we got back, everybody had been very worried. The chopper had dropped below the radio level, and they had lost contact. They thought the plane had gone down. That one makes me shudder even today.

Life and work were moving along, and as the weeks passed, we always had a full load of patients but we were not over-whelmed. It was getting hot, with an ocean breeze that cooled it a little, most of the time. Sleeping day or night was difficult because of the heat. I had a fan that blew across the bed, blowing the sheet up and down. That usually helped. The bugs were not quite so bad- but I still looked in my shoes before putting them on. Better safe than sorry.

Finally, I was to report to the wards in the morning. I was not really looking forward to it. I thought I would be bored. I was wrong.

# CHAPTER 21

## The Wards

It was my turn to rotate to the wards. It was hot, and I had just lost my air-conditioned work-place. I had spoken to the nurse in charge of the wards and learned what the duties were, and it seemed fairly straight-forward. There were a lot of patients in the seven wards. Each ward was staffed with a corpsman, The patients were separated by what was wrong with them. Patients with medical problems were on one ward; most of the patients were surgical or orthopedic and most had been in ICU/RR. One ward on the end held overflow patients, and prisoners when we had them.

My job was to watch for problems and to collect the daily twenty-four hour report. "Watch for problems" is non-specific, but with seven wards and about eighteen young male patients per ward, plus a young male corpsman in charge, stuff just happens.

My concern was for the medical stuff that could happen. My first night of duty, my plan was to make rounds on all the wards to see who was there and how they were doing; that way, I would get to know where the problems might be. So I went from ward to ward talking to the patients, checking dressings, asking about pain levels, checking casts, and testing circulation in toes and fingers. That took a long time, and I realized that I did not need to do that. After that first night, all I did was ask the corpsman what the problems were and check those. I had a lot of respect for the corpsmen. They did well. I would spot-check other patients, like new arrivals from the ICU.

In the ICU/RR all medications were given in an IV. When the patient got transferred to the ward, the IV was pulled, so that avenue was gone. On the wards, all the medications were oral or IM (intramuscular). A few of the patients were still on large doses of penicillin, so the drug had to be given in a shot into the large butt muscle (gluteus) twice a day.

At about 2200, one of the corpsmen stopped me and told me the shots were ready to give. I looked at him strangely and said "Aren't you trained to do that?" I knew that 9-Bs were trained to be field medics, give injections, start IVs, and so forth. He said, "Yes, but the other nurse liked to do that herself." I said, "Well, I don't. Let's get started." His eyes sparkled, and he broke out in an unbelievable grin, as he picked up the tray of medications and we went to the first patient. I watched him check the patient's name against the medication card, have the patient turn over, he measured from the hip bone, and gave the shot flawlessly. I left him to give the rest. I went on to the other wards to do the same thing. Word travelled fast. By the time I finished on two wards, the corpsmen were greeting me with smiles, standing by their tray of injections.

These young corpsmen were working in a hospital today. Next week they could be assigned to a field unit in combat. It was vital to keep their skills up. I was excited that I just figured out what my job was--teacher and it and it was going to be fun.

Over the next few weeks, it got hotter and more humid. Sleeping was off and on, and usually from exhaustion. Everything was sticky. Humidity would get to a point, the rain would pour down in buckets for a while, and then it would go away, leaving the air clear and cool. Then the cycle would start again. As I said before, the wards did not have walls, just screens from about three feet off of the ground and then up about five feet. After that the solid wall met the roof.

This particular day, I was on the day shift, it was about dinner-time, and the rain started along with a hefty wind blowing the rain into the wards from the north side. We had a bunch of casted patients right in its pathway. There was nowhere to move the beds. I grabbed some blankets, a chair, a hammer, and some nails. This was a downpour I could hardly see through. I was teetering on a chair with water running in rivers and rivulets from my head down, as I was hanging blankets over the screens to keep the patients dry. I was soaked to my skin in seconds. The patients were loving every minute of this drama/ comedy and said so, trying not to laugh, when I finished and went back into the ward looking like a drowned rat. The plaster casts got lightly sprinkled and not damaged.

One of my jobs was to count patients to be sure the census was correct when I turned in my daily twenty-four hour report from each ward. I got to the ward that held the prisoners and counted one, two, three, four, five and started to write that on my form. The guard stopped me and said, "I don't know what you are counting, ma'am, but there are four more under the bed." I looked at him and bent to look under the bed to see four kids with very large eyes staring back at me. My first thought was, *"What do I do about this"* My second thought was, *"Somebody brought them here. It can be handled in the morning."* They had what they needed for the moment -blankets, pillows. I told the guard to call me if he needed any help.

The days kept moving along. The heat was unchanging, although it did cool off at night a little. The humidity stayed the same. One morning, leaving work, I heard the familiar, hair-raising, soul--stirring sound of multiple choppers heading in our direction. I knew it would be a few hours before the current crew needed any help, so I ate breakfast and went to catch a few hours of sleep. It felt good to be out of the ICU/RR, where every patient was acute, needing instant and constant care.

# CHAPTER 22

## The Push - Chu Lai

This was only the second big mass casualty event during my tour, but it was two too many. We had many events that seemed like mass casualties but were just very busy days. I woke up about 1400 to the sound of another chopper. They had been coming at intervals all day. I got up, grabbed a quick snack, and started making the rounds of who needed help. ICU/RR was holding it's own; triage was busy but seemed to be under control. I poked my head into The Central Material Section(CMS) where all the sets are cleaned and sterilized for the operating room. The sink was piled high with bloody instruments, basins, and other odd items. Two men were in the back working hard to keep up with the operating room needs for sterile packs. Even though they had charts for putting a set together with all the required scissors, basins, and clamps, wrapping them and then sterilizing them takes time. So, I washed dishes for a while to help them catch up. One man, looking very hot and stressed, poked his head out to see what the noise was. Sweat was running down his forehead and dripping on the floor. He looked at me with a little relief in his eyes, straightened up a bit and went back to his task.

Finishing up there, I went to the mess hall for dinner and then early to the wards to see who the new patients were. The medical ward had a few new patients by then- two with malaria. These men needed to be watched for the fevers that come in the acute phase, with a dramatic shaking chill. The temperature can quickly climb to 105 degrees Fahrenheit, a critical state. One of them was unstable. He had to be sent by chopper to 3rd Field Hospital in Saigon due to complications from malaria. He started peeing blood. Not a good sign.

The ward had about fifteen patients. Most needed antibiotics for such things as foot infections or other infected wounds that were trauma, not surgical. Medical problems sidelined quite a few troops.

One young man came to the ward walking when guided but not responding to questions. He was hugging his helmet. He was clearly in shock, he had the thousand-yard stare. He would not release the helmet or acknowledge the existence of anyone. We put him to bed, helmet and all, on the medical ward and just watched him for a while. He started responding twenty-four hours later. We found out that the dent in his helmet was made by an enemy round. The helmet saved his life. He willingly went back to duty after a couple of days' rest.

Most of the patients were orthopedic or surgical and went to one of those wards. I paid special attention to the new arrivals on each ward and asked the corpsman if he needed help with anyone, as they were not long out of the operating room and could have problems. Together we looked at some of the sicker new patients and discussed what kind of problems to look for: swelling, bleeding, excessive pain, for example. I checked toes and fingers on a few of the casted ones, dressings on some of the surgical ones. All seemed to be doing well. These wards were getting full. Luckily, we had an overflow ward of mixed surgical patients.

I did go up to the ICU a couple of times and help with one or two of the more complicated patients that needed one-on-one care, when needed. I walked through triage to help when needed and checked in CMS for dirty dishes. The day progressed and was soon over, and cleanup started again.

I missed the action in the ICU/RR, but I did not miss the constant adrenalin rush... well, maybe a little. Out here by the beach, I could watch the sun rise over the South China Sea. It was always beautiful.

# CHAPTER 23

## Out to Lunch

One night during a lull, just before sunrise, I was standing on the back porch of one of the wards, just enjoying the tropical breeze, listening to the surf, and daydreaming of other places and times. I looked up and saw a light out in the water coming toward us. As the light neared and the sun started to rise, the light became many lights and then itbecame a ship. It was the *USS Repose*, a Navy hospital ship that was sailing up and down the coast. It had a large red cross painted on the side.

I reported out to the oncoming nurse and went to breakfast. Sitting in the mess hall, I started talking about the *Repose* with other nurses. I decided that I would really like to visit that ship. I used to be a Navy nurse, and really felt that I should see the inside of that ship to see what I may be missing.

Finished with breakfast, I went through the dish-washing routine, scraping, and dunking my tray in suds and then in boiling water. On my way back to my hooch, I stopped to see the chief nurse and told her what I saw that morning. She already knew it was there. They had been in contact with the captain wanting to send a critically ill patient out to their ICU. I said, quickly, "Can I go too?" I would love to visit that ship." She said, "Let me check." She came back and said, "The captain has invited us out for lunch and a tour of the ship." He will be sending a helicopter at 1100 hour. "I eagerly said yes. And then for an instant wondered what to wear. That was dumb. I had fatigues and fatigues. I went back to my hooch, took a two-hour nap, got up, cleaned up, put on a clean set of fatigues, and hurried down to the office to join the chief nurse and two other nurses for our lunch on the *USS Repose*.

The Navy chopper arrived on our helipad sharply at 1100 hours. The crewmen opened the door of the chopper, hopped out, saluted, and helped us into the chopper and our seats. We strapped on seatbelts and head-sets and took off listening to the chatter of the pilots and the ship radio operator. We landed gracefully on the helipad of the ship, got out, and were led down a flight of steps (actually a ladder) to hallways around turns and through doors (hatches). It was a maze; we had to keep ducking and stepping over things. We arrived at the officer's mess, where we met our tour guide. We would meet the captain and the chief nurse later.

The tour guide was a nurse, a lieutenant, dressed in a pristine starched white uniform with nurse's cap, white nylons, and white shoes, which were polished. She told us a little about the ship's history, where it had been, and what it was capable of doing in the way of patient care. As we toured through the wards and support facilities like CMS and the kitchen, I was impressed at how clean the whole place was. In fact, I was beginning to feel a little like the *Peanuts* character "Pig Pen" in my fatigues with changed dirt. The patients had white sheets instead of the slightly brown ones we used. The corpsmen and nurses dressed in starched whites, and the walls were gray-white. The one thing that stuck out the most was the fact that nothing was movable. The patient beds were attached to the bulkhead (wall). All the tables, equipment, and chairs were also attached. Not good for patient access, but I guess when the ship floats on the ocean, things tend to move unless tied down.

The tour over, we headed back to the officer's mess for lunch. I looked at the neatly set table with a white tablecloth, white china plates, and actual silver silverware lining both sides of the plate. There were several forks (none with bent tines) on the left, and a knife and two spoons on the right. The waiters came in with menus to take our orders. I don't remember what the choices were because I was in total awe by now. Please remember my description of meals in our Army mess hall. None of our choices were reconstituted. The captain and chief nurse were very nice, and the conversation was good. When it became time to leave, we all expressed ourappreciation, said our good-byes, and headed for the captain's chopper for the trip back.

I headed back to what was home for us with mixed feelings. I was overwhelmed by how nice and comfortable it was, even if very formal. I finally decided that I was happy where I was. If I must go to war, I don't want to wear a starched white uniform and panty-hose, and I would not be happy working in a place where I could not move anything for better patient access. I rationalized that well. It was a beautiful ship - clean, no bugs, and good food. I sighed and had, I'm sure, a distant look in my eyes.

Oh, and the patient did get to the ship in an Army Medivac helicopter with a doctor and nurse and medical gear, oxygen, suction, and so forth. He did make it home. A trip to Third Field in Saigon was ruled out because the patient was critical and would not have made it that far.

It was getting to be late summer, and my tour in Vietnam was coming to a close. I was still enjoying the ease of work on the wards. The corpsmen were great, and the convalescing patients were fun. All the problems I saw were solvable. Some, I made an effort not to see because they were silly. These were bored, injured young men. Young men just do things.

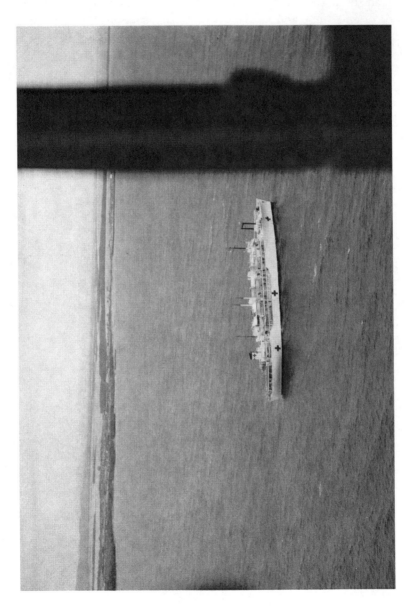

Hospital Ship

# CHAPTER 24

## Going Home

The summer passed with not much change activity. The hospital stayed moderate to very busy all the time. Early on one cool, humid, mid-September morning, the hospital had been quiet for over twenty-four hours. The nurses and corpsmen had finished the cleanup process after the last group of patients and were now enjoying a much-needed rest. Three of us, Elly, Betty, and I, were at the end of our tour. We had arrived at the same time in 1966, almost a year ago. It had been a hectic year. Now, though we were sad to leave our friends behind, we were ready to go home.

We sat in our hooch, too tired to do anything else, remembering all the things we had done in just a year. We had helped to treat a lot of wounded soldiers and Vietnamese civilians and at times worked more than twenty-four hours at a stretch. The hospital had moved once. We looked at each other and discussed how we had grown as nurses and people, and then we gave passing thought to how we would adjust to being home. None of us had driven a car, watched television, worn decent clothes, eaten a McDonald's burger, or shopped in a real store for over a year. How would we deal with the anti-war atmosphere that dominated home newspapers and *Time* magazine? We had lived with extreme emotional ups and downs for a year and longed for the normalcy of home.

During this deep, heady discussion, the company clerk burst into the hooch and announced, "If you can be ready in an hour, you can leave today!" We started moving before the clerk was out the door. "And," he turned to say, "stop by headquarters for your orders." From lounge clothes to uniforms, bags packed, goodbyes to friends, checkout, and orders, we were on the tarmac in fifty-six minutes. The flight crew tossed our bags into the airplane, and we were airborne in route to Cam Ranh Bay to await our flight home.

We reported into the housing office at Cam Ranh Bay about 3 p.m. and picked up our room assignments for the night. Our flight was tentatively scheduled to leave at about ten the next morning. Restless after dinner, we started walking around the base. We found a spot to sit and watch the planes take off and land. Cam Ranh Bay had a large landing strip, so it was an entry and exit point for troops and supplies. A large Continental jet was lumbering toward the runway with a load of soldiers going home. As it edged toward the take-off position, we could see puffs of smoke landing on the strip. Curious, we watched for a second and then gasped in horror. The Viet Cong were shelling the runway. Before they could find their range and hit the airplane, that civilian pilot saw the incoming fire. He must have given the plane full power because he used a very short strip of runway, and took off at a steep angle that almost banged the tail on the way up. We looked at each other wide-eyed and speechless, hesitated for a moment, and then hurried back to our rooms for what turned out to be a very long, anxious night.

The next morning, we were up early, had breakfast in the mess hall, and headed for flight operations. Our flight was on schedule. We looked around the crowded room, saw soldiers dozing propped on duffel bags, draped over chairs, reading, or just staring into space. We joined the group to sit and wait. Finally, our flight was called. People stirred and quietly lined up. No one hurried, crowded, or got impatient-in fact, no one said anything. The plane was full. We were packed into seats lined up four across on each side, but no one seemed to care. The three of us found seats together, shoved our carry-on bags into the overhead bin, and sat. Others busied themselves getting comfortable in their seats for the long ride.

The flight made one stop in Japan for fuel and continued toward Seattle. Seattle International Airport runways were also used by McCord Air Force Base air traffic. I do not remember how many hours passed. The pilot would say something every now and then about the weather or turbulence. The flight attendants tried to provide a small amount of service, and people took what they offered, quietly ate, and went back to sleep. This was a plane-load of young men and three female nurses. No one said anything. The silence filled the airplane. We had survived a year in a war zone, and I silently hoped the plane would make it home safely. I did not want to think about the alternative.

When the pilot announced our approach to Seattle, a few people stirred, buckled seat-belts, and adjusted seat-backs. I could see lights out the window. I jumped when the landing gear went down and locked and held my breath as we neared the ground. With the first bump of the wheels touching the ground, one man let out a "whoop," and everyone came alive at once. They shouted, tossed hats in the air, hugged, pounded each other, stomped, and yelled. We were back in "the world." We had survived the first step in the coming home process. What would follow was still unknown, but for now, we were happy.

A calm, deep, male voice over the intercom announced, "Welcome home."

# CHAPTER 25

## Home Again

The three of us walked to the baggage claim to get our luggage. We got swept up into a gaggle of people heading the same way. People in a hurry walked around us like we were not there. They were having conversations about normal things-business, golf, sports, and family. The war in Vietnam did not exist for them. I was overwhelmed by the ambient noise, TVs, overhead announcements, lights, and high-energy activity. The barrage of lights of all different colors were all enticing me to buy something or do something. I reacted to all of it. It was draining. I was used to reacting to every noise. I had to relearn to ignore the ones I did not want or need to hear.

At baggage claim, we waited for our duffel bags to come out of the chute. All the duffel bags looked the same, so I do not remember how I got the right one, but I did. The three of us said our goodbyes and parted company to find our flights out, the next leg to home. Ellie and Betty were both from the East Coast. We had paid flights to our home of record or next duty station. It was early evening; my flight would go out the next day. I stayed the night in a nearby motel and would leave the next morning. That set up, I called my family and told them I was home safely but still in Seattle. I would be arriving in the morning and gave them the flight number and time.

I got to the hotel. I was again, very glad to be taking off my uniform after an incredibly long flight. I took a long, hot shower, lay down on the bed, and turned the television on, this was the first TV program I had seen in a year. I don't remember what it was, but it seemed silly. I heard noises in the hallway. A man ran down the hall knocking on doors, yelling "Welcome home party in 203!" I groaned, I was not going to get involved in that mess. I turned off the TV and thought for a while before going to sleep. I thought about home, about what

I had to do to get resettled, but most of all I thought about what really mattered in life, and it wasn't *things*. I had lived for a year without all the trappings of civilization. I clearly did not need them to survive. Now I was surrounded by things, and it was confusing.

I did not get out of the Army; I decided to make it a career. I had a month's leave before going back to work. I was reassigned to Madigan Army Medical Center in Tacoma, Washington. That would come soon enough. Now I had to get myself back together. My car had been in storage for a year. I had to get it fixed up and running. I had very little in the way of household goods. Clothing and boxed personal items had been stored with my family.

I got an early flight the next day – the last leg of my trip. The flight landed safely in Sacramento, and my family members were there to pick me up. We loaded my baggage, and off we went. Riding in a car felt strange. After the "how was your trip" comments, and a return of "how have you all been," we were home. Strangely awkward. We had been in two different worlds with no bridge between them. Even though I had written letters home frequently, they did not understand, nor could they. The war in Vietnam was not real or personal. I later found out that my father had put my picture up on the bulletin board at work, along with the other men who put up pictures of their sons. That was special.

I was way out of step in their world. I could not talk about the latest TV programs, grocery and food items, clothing, movies, and so forth. I was not up on the latest fast-food places or sports teams, etc. The things I valued had changed. My frame of reference was Vietnam, and nobody wanted to hear about it. I decided to forget about it, enjoy my vacation, see and do a few things, and catch up on everything I missed, including ice cream, television, and hamburgers. In that sense, it felt great to be home.

Someone helped me pick up my car and get it going. It needed new battery and a lube job. Driving it for the first time was pretty scary. I drove twenty-five miles an hour on the freeway at first. Cars were going seventy around me. It took a while to get used to the fast pace. I got all my boxes together to see what I had and what I needed. I went shopping for clothing. All my white nurse uniforms had been boxed for a year. I would mail those to my next duty station, and they would hold them until I got there. I had to get my finances together. I had saved a big part of my check every month, so I had several thousand dollars saved up for whatever I needed. It was going to be nice to get my life back together and get into my own home again. Vacation was over faster than I wanted it to be.

I packed all my things into my Karman Ghia and headed north to Tacoma, Washington, and Madigan Army Medical Center to begin the rest of my life.

My twenty-eight year Army career took me to Europe and many great places in this country. Some were, maybe, not so great, but it balanced out. All that time, Vietnam was pushed back in my mind and all but forgotten. No one really ever spoke about it. It did not come up. I was busy with new and exciting things. My Vietnam service did follow me, though. At one duty station, I was spit at because of the post sticker on my car. While I was stationed in Berlin, Germany, the Wall was still up. Friends and I went through Check Point Charlie to shop and/or just look around. I was at the cash register of one of the shops buying something. Right by my left elbow was a coin-drop box, much like the March of Dimes boxes, only this one said "Aid to North Vietnam." It was written in English. Americans were the obvious targeted recipients. No, I did not drop coins in the box.

I retired in 1990 and came home to California. It was then, children of Vietnam veterans started asking about the war and wanted to know what happened to their fathers. I shared my experience with high schoolers and some college kids. I even developed a slide presentation that I still give at luncheons.

In 2011, I was diagnosed with cancer in my right lung. It was a very rare cancer presumed to be caused by Agent Orange. The cancer was removed and has been in remission. I am cancer-free, but not pain-free.

The much-discussed issue of PTSD(Post-traumatic stress disorder) in Vietnam veterans is ongoing. Those of us who made the Army a career had peer support and did much better than those who got out and went back home looking for the same world they left. Many are still seeking treatment today.

I am proud to have served my country as an Army nurse, and I am proud to have served in Vietnam. I would still be serving if I could. Today I am a veteran's' advocate in the California State Legislature representing the Military Officers Association of America. After September 11, 2011, I saw veterans coming home again receiving basically the same treatment I received coming home from Vietnam. The Middle East veterans were, at least, welcomed home, but then they were forgotten again. As a group, the veterans'organizations, mine included, work to make sure the new veterans are not forgotten.

CPSIA information can be obtained
at www.ICGtesting.com
Printed in the USA
LVOW12s1641110118
562712LV00003B/605/P